HELPING SKILLS FOR
SOCIAL WORK
DIRECT PRACTICE

Helping Skills for Social Work Direct Practice

Jacqueline Corcoran, Ph.D.

OXFORD
UNIVERSITY PRESS

OXFORD
UNIVERSITY PRESS

Published in the United States of America by Oxford University Press, Inc.,
198 Madison Avenue, New York, NY, 10016
United States of America

Oxford University Press, Inc. publishes works that further Oxford University's
objective of excellence in research, scholarship, and education

Oxford is a registered trade mark of Oxford University Press in the UK
and in certain other countries

Library of Congress Cataloging-in-Publication Data

Corcoran, Jacqueline.
Helping skills for social work direct practice / Jacqueline Corcoran.
p. cm.
Includes bibliographical references and index.
ISBN 978-0-19-973483-2 (pbk. : alk. paper)
1. Social service. 2. Counselor and client. 3. Solution-focused therapy.
4. Social service—Case studies. 5. Counselor and client—Case studies.
6. Solution-focused therapy—Case studies. I. Title.
HV40.C673 2012
361.3'2—dc23   2011017465

Typeset in Arno Pro

Since the Northern Virginia Campus of the Virginia Commonwealth University School of Social Work will close in Spring 2011, I would like to dedicate this book to all the students I have taught and advised at this campus for the last ten years.

CONTENTS

PART FOUR: GOAL SETTING AND INTERVENTION

PART FIVE: EVALUATION AND TERMINATION

PART SIX: ETHICS

ACKNOWLEDGMENTS

To my fellow chapter authors, Melisa Atkeson, Emily Brown, William Hayden, and Bryan Norman, I thank you for all your hard work and the contributions you made to this volume. Likewise, to all the students who contributed case examples, I truly appreciate your sharing so that other students can learn: Eileen Abedejos, Farjana Akhter, Jody Baumstein, Freda Botwe, Meagan Bullock, Morgan Chiti, Laura Cook, Colleen Dorgan, Kristen Durbin, Paula Durman, Erika Deem, Kelly Frederickson, Debbie Fuller, Frances, Gallagher, Gladys Garibaldi, Eleni Hadjichristodoulou, Elaine Harrington, Laura Harty, Jessica Jenkins, Lisa Katerman, Courtney Kraft, Marguerite Lawless, Annie Le, Laura Luna, Laura Macone, Nazia Mirza, Lindsay Nisbett, Nicole O'Connor, Julia Richardson, Michele Roberts, Tanya Sanders, Shayna Sargent, Andrea Saevoon, Anne Strozeski, and Bianchinetta Suarez.

Thank you also to the social work editorial team at Oxford, editor Maura Roessner and her assistant Nicholas Liu, who are always gracious and helpful at every turn in the process, from proposal to final product.

A final acknowledgment goes to my father Patrick Corcoran for his painstaking efforts at proofreading and indexing so that we could put forward the best product possible.

HELPING SKILLS FOR SOCIAL WORK DIRECT PRACTICE

PART 1

INTRODUCTION

INTRODUCTION AND OVERVIEW

The target audiences for *Helping Skills for Social Work Direct Practice* are bachelor's and master's degree students taking courses in direct practice. Direct practice focuses on helping skills enacted in a one-to-one fashion in individual and family modalities, known in social work terms as the *micro* level of practice.

Helping Skills for Social Work Direct Practice is organized around a framework that has a long tradition in social work, the problem-solving process (Perlman, 1957). The problem-solving process comprises the following phases of helping:

1. engagement
2. assessment of problems and strengths
3. goal setting
4. intervention
5. evaluation and termination

The book moves through the phases in order, helping you to understand which techniques to apply at what stages. Along with short descriptions of the techniques, an abundance of examples and exercises provide students with many opportunities to apply the particular skill to practice scenarios drawn from actual student process recordings. In this way, you will be able to learn to use the techniques through practice and apply them to the clients with whom you work. Illustrations are de-identified and are selected from many different fields of social work practice:

- child welfare
- health
- mental health
- children and schools
- partner violence
- addictions
- gerontological practice

Cases will show social workers and interns enacting a variety of roles, including:

- case manager
- caseworker
- crisis counselor
- hospital social worker
- school social worker

Note that "therapist" is *not* one of the roles, as direct practice in social work is much more broadly defined than the provision of psychotherapy, and the focus in the Bachelor's in Social Work and the first year of the Master's in Social Work program is on these other direct practice roles. However, this book *will* teach you how to be therapeutic—working collaboratively to support people's efforts to cope with difficult life events and to change these circumstances, and to make changes in their behaviors and their relationships that will help alter their circumstances—in the variety of settings to which foundation students are assigned.

The examples and exercises in the book utilize diverse settings and roles that will help students generalize the skills to different practice settings and client problems. Furthermore, socially diverse clients are represented in the examples: children, older adults, people from low socioeconomic strata and from a variety of ethnic groups. An instructor's manual accompanies *Helping Skills for Social Work Direct Practice* with answers provided. Therefore, the chief focus of *Helping Skills for Social Work Direct Practice* is on the application of skills through an abundance of examples so that students can see how direct practice in social work is carried out and exercises to allow students to practice what they will deliver in their work.

The skills building is primarily applied to individual work with clients, but special considerations for working with families are also covered. Family social work is defined as work "with any part of the family system. . . where membership in the family is a concern, or where the family or some part of the family system is the target for change" (Yanca & Johnson, 2008). In the National Association of Social Workers Code of Ethics, the importance of human relationships is emphasized as a core value of the profession (NASW, 1999). Social workers not only provide a relationship to clients, they also work to build and enhance the naturally existing relationships in clients' lives.

Many of the same techniques and skills used in working with individuals apply to group work, so the same helping process can be followed. Although some examples derive from group work, *Helping Skills for Social Work Direct Practice* will not delve deeply into group work, as special considerations must be paid to group dynamics, and particular skills are needed for effectively facilitating a group. The reader interested in a workbook-style format for group work may reference Corcoran (2009).

THEORETICAL UNDERPINNING

Helping Skills for Social Work Direct Practice uses two models of helping: motivational interviewing and solution-focused therapy. These overlay the framework of the problem-solving process—the solid foundation of basic helping skills, such as open-ended questions and reflecting statements. The integration of motivational interviewing and solution-focused therapy is described in detail in the book *Building Strengths and Skills* (Corcoran, 2005), but here it will be applied to social work's problem-solving process and will focus primarily on the application of these techniques and skills. The main thrust is that working with client problems and limitations, as well as client strengths, is needed to optimally help clients (McMillen, Morris, & Sherraden, 2004). Along with learning basic helping skills, students will be introduced to the techniques used in Motivational Interviewing (MI) and Solution-Focused Therapy (SFT) and will be given ample opportunity to put these into action.

In the following sections, the strengths-based models solution-focused therapy and motivational interviewing, presented in *Helping skills for Social Work Direct Practice* are elaborated upon. Exhibit 1 shows how these models are integrated within the problem-solving process. Future chapters will illustrate how these are applied, as there is a chapter devoted to each stage of the problem-solving process. The final chapter of the book will demonstrate how the values and ethical principles and standards of social work can be operationalized in a variety of practice settings.

SOLUTION-FOCUSED THERAPY

Developed by deShazer, Berg, and colleagues (Berg, 1994; Berg & Miller, 1992; Cade & O'Hanlon, 1993; de Shazer, Berg, Lipchick, Nunnally, Molnar, Gingerich, & Weiner-Davis, 1986; O'Hanlon & Weiner-Davis, 1989), solution-focused therapy (SFT) emphasizes the strengths people bring and how these can be applied to the change process. Clients are

EXHIBIT 1: Stages of the Helping Process and Techniques		
Stage of the Helping Process	Model	Techniques
Engagement	SFT	Orienting toward goals and strengths Coping questions Normalizing Reframing Relationship questions
Assessment: Exploration of the Problem	MI	Exploring the advantages and disadvantages of the problem behavior
Exploration of the Solution	SFT	Exception finding Strengths finding
Goal Setting and Implementation of the Plan	SFT	Future-oriented questioning Scaling intervention Problem solving and coming up with ideas for change Providing information collaboratively Handling noncompliance
Evaluation and Termination	SFT	Scaling questions Termination questions

assumed to have the capability to solve their own problems through resources that are found by eliciting and exploring times when the problem does not exert its negative influence and/or when the client has coped successfully.

Rather than focusing on the past and the history of the problem, using SFT, the attention orients on a future without the problem as a way to build vision, hope, and motivation for the client. Extensive historical information is not viewed as necessary in SFT since understanding the past will not change the future without action. The past is explored only through the process of exception finding, identifying the times when problems do not occur. The focus of conversation between the practitioner and the client moves to how these exceptions can be applied in the future.

The assumption in solution-focused therapy is that change occurs in a systemic way. A small change is all that is necessary to create a "spiral effect": the client takes a step in the right direction, others in the context respond differently, and the client feels more empowered and is encouraged toward further change. Behaving differently *and* thinking differently are part of the processes of change (de Shazer, 1994). Rapid change is possible; all that is necessary in treatment is for a small change to occur, as this will reverberate throughout the system.

Solution-focused therapy values individuals for their unique perspective and assumes their right to determine their own goals. Clients are encouraged to find the solutions that fit their own worldview. The practitioner works collaboratively with the client to build the client's awareness of strengths. These strengths are then mobilized and applied to problem situations.

Solution-focused techniques build upon people's existing problem-solving capacities to create change by focusing on concrete goals that can be achieved in a brief time frame. The focus on client resources and what the client is *doing right* empowers and offers hope to people who are often beleaguered by the time they come to a social worker for assistance. Solution-focused therapy holds many advantages for social work in a broad variety of settings and offers a method by which to operationalize core values and principles of social work. These include the following:

- the importance of context for behavior (in SFT, the assumption is that *context and interpersonal interactions,* more than factors within the individual, drive behavior)
- a systemic perspective (i.e., change in one part of the system can invoke change in another part of the system)
- client self-determination (clients have a right to choose their own goals and solutions, taking into consideration their unique resources and situations)
- a focus on strengths and resources of the individual

Solution-focused techniques also operationalize social workers' ethical responsibility to clients in terms of understanding, and being sensitive to, clients' diverse social backgrounds: ethnicity, immigration status, gender, sexual orientation, age, marital status, political beliefs, and disability (NASW Code of Ethics, 1999). When discussing how to work with clients from other cultures, the literature frequently mentions "the importance of incorporating a client's worldview, empowering the client, and utilizing a client's strengths in cross-cultural social work practice" (Lee, 2003, p. 387). Lee explores the ways in which solution-focused therapy operationalizes these ideas, including emphasizing collaborative work with clients, eliciting and building upon client strengths, and helping clients find solutions that fit within their worldview. A short-term, goal-focused approach that attends to interactional patterns and context, rather than individual dynamics, also makes solution-focused therapy compatible with the worldview of clients from many ethnic minority backgrounds. Social diversity is further discussed in Chapter 12 on ethics and values.

In *Helping Skills for Social Work Direct Practice*, solution-focused therapy is used throughout the phases of the problem-solving process, but especially during engagement, goal setting, and strengths finding. SFT has a unique emphasis on assessing the client's relationship to the change process. Many of the clients seen in settings where social workers are employed are there involuntarily. Some of them are formally mandated by the court system to receive intervention. Others may be nonvoluntary in the sense that they feel coerced to seek help by a family member, romantic partner, or another system such as school or child protective services. In a way that conveys respect for the value and dignity of the person (NASW, 1999), solution-focused work places the onus on the client so that he or she is responsible for the process of change.

MOTIVATIONAL INTERVIEWING

Developed over the last 20 years (Dunn, Deroo, & Rivara, 2001), motivational interviewing is "a client-centered, directive method for enhancing intrinsic motivation to change by exploring and resolving ambivalence" (Miller & Rollnick, 2002, p. 25). Originally for the treatment of substance abuse, motivational interviewing (MI) is now being applied to other areas of change, such as diet and exercise (Moyers & Rollnick, 2002). It has been employed as both a standalone treatment and a way to engage people in other intervention approaches (Walitzer, Dermen, & Conners, 1999). Several guiding principles underlie the techniques of motivational interviewing:

- expressing empathy
- identifying discrepancy between the clients' problematic behavior and their goals for themselves and their loved ones
- rolling with resistance
- supporting self-efficacy
- developing a change plan

These principles establish motivational interviewing as a collaborative model. Even when talking with people about difficult topics—their illegal, dangerous, or harmful behavior—techniques pave the way so the practitioner can stay attuned to the client's position while also guiding the client toward change.

Empathic listening and affirming statements are foundational techniques of motivational interviewing. While these techniques are drawn from nondirective counseling (Rogers, 1951), the two methods differ in several key ways. Nondirective counseling allows the client to decide the content and direction of the discussion. In motivational interviewing, the practitioner systematically directs the process toward building client motivation.

Another difference between the approaches has to do with the use of empathy. In contrast to nondirective counseling in which empathic reflection is used regardless of the direction the client is headed, empathy in motivational interviewing is employed to reinforce client statements about changing. In social work, we tackle challenging problems, such as child abuse, criminal offenses, anger problems, and substance abuse, and many of our populations include nonvoluntary clients. Motivational interviewing can help us negotiate conversations about these difficult problems while remaining respectful, collaborative, and change-oriented—all at the same time. Some of the dos and don'ts of motivational interviewing are expressed in Exhibit 2:

The principles of motivational interviewing are enacted through the following techniques:

- listening reflectively and demonstrating empathy
- eliciting self-motivational statements
- handling resistance
- enacting a decisional balance

These techniques are selectively presented in *Helping Skills for Social Work Direct Practice* as they apply to beginning practice situations that interns and new social workers may encounter.

EXHIBIT 2: **Guidelines for Motivational Interviewing**

Do:
1. Set a tentative agenda, allowing for flexibility.
2. Begin where the client is.
3. Explore and reflect the client's perceptions.
4. Use empathic reflection selectively when clients express reasons to change.
5. Reflect by making paraphrasing and summarizing statements rather than using questions.
6. Use affirmation and positive reframing of the client's statements to bolster self-efficacy.
7. Present a brief summary at the end of each contact.
8. Use phrases like "I wonder if. . ." and "some people find. . ." to probe about problem behaviors gently.

Don't:
1. Argue, lecture, confront, or persuade.
2. Moralize, criticize, preach, or judge.
3. Give expert advice at the beginning.
4. Order, direct, warn, or threaten.
5. Do most of the talking.
6. Debate about diagnostic labeling.
7. Ask closed-ended questions.
8. Ask a lot of questions (more than three in a row) without reflecting.
9. Offer advice and feedback until later stages when sufficient motivation has been built.

(Adapted from Miller & Rollnick, 2002; Killick & Allen, 1997)

CONCLUSION

Helping Skills for Social Work Direct Practice uses two models of helping, motivational interviewing and solution-focused therapy, while at the same time pulling from a solid foundation of basic helping skills such as open-ended questions and reflecting statements. These models are supported by the framework of the problem-solving process:

1. engagement
2. assessment
3. goal setting
4. intervention
5. evaluation and termination

Helping Skills for Social Work Direct Practice presents, with an abundance of examples and exercises, real case situations involving clients from socially diverse backgrounds who are seen by social work students and beginning practitioners in a variety of practice types. The diversity in the book's examples not only increases students' likelihood to identify with the material and to generalize skills, it also exposes the reader to the broad range of roles and settings with which social work is involved. This workbook stands apart from other direct practice texts in its emphasis on the acquisition of skills that are then applied in a concrete way. Other books tend to offer discussion about social work's values and principles, but lack direction or examples of how to actually *do* social work while enacting its values and principles in client situations that arise in everyday practice. *That* is this book's goal.

PART 2

ENGAGEMENT

CHAPTER 1

MEETING CLIENTS

This chapter discusses a social worker's first meetings with clients. It addresses what to say, how to introduce yourself, and how to engage with more than one person when working with a family. The chapter includes home visiting, as social workers often conduct their business with clients not in an office setting, but in the places where clients live their lives. At the conclusion of the chapter, you will hopefully feel more comfortable and better prepared to begin meeting with clients.

INTRODUCTIONS

When you introduce yourself to clients, use your first and last name, but use the client's formal title (e.g., Mr. Hernandez) unless you are asked to refer to the person by first name. When working with a family, however, always continue to use the parent's formal title (Mr. or Mrs.) or refer to them by role ("Dad" or "Mom") in the presence of their children. These salutations convey respect for the authority of the parent and give the message to both parents and children that we recognize that the parents are in charge of their children.

Before you can tell clients the reason you are meeting with them, *you* have to know the reason you are meeting with them. Sometimes interns identify the purpose of a meeting as "to build rapport with," "to check in with," or "to get to know" the clients. While these are important first steps, all work with clients should have direction beyond this. In addition to defining a purpose for your work with a client overall, you should define the purpose of each contact and make this explicit to the client. This is particularly important when working with people who are mandated to attend services, as they can become understandably frustrated if they believe professionals are simply taking up their time without direction. Further, social workers are often involved with vulnerable and oppressed populations. If contacts are random and purposeless, a social worker could inadvertently contribute to feelings of powerlessness that these clients may already feel.

A further aspect of establishing a purpose is to strive for a collaborative tone. You don't want to indicate that you will be "doing for" or "doing to" the client. Instead, you can allude to the work that you will be doing together, as in: "*We* can talk and work together to make changes that you're interested in."

A time frame, when possible, could be attached to the purpose of the work, as in, "We will be meeting for four weeks to decide what services will be put in place for your children," "until we agree that you have met your goals," or "I wanted to visit with you once more to see how the plan we talked about is going." At times, you might be meeting a client who has already worked with other helpers. You may be taking over the client's case from another worker or helping another worker manage his or her caseload. To establish a purpose for your work, you can reference the services the client received in the past, ask about his or her understanding of the previous work, and clear up misperceptions that may exist about what you will be doing together. You can go even further by asking "what was helpful?" and "what was not so helpful?" about the previous work to convey to clients that they are the experts on what is useful for them (de Jong & Berg, 2008) and that you are interested in their perspectives and experiences.

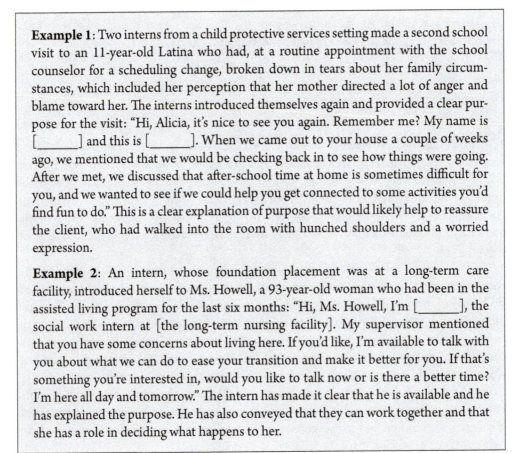

Example 1: Two interns from a child protective services setting made a second school visit to an 11-year-old Latina who had, at a routine appointment with the school counselor for a scheduling change, broken down in tears about her family circumstances, which included her perception that her mother directed a lot of anger and blame toward her. The interns introduced themselves again and provided a clear purpose for the visit: "Hi, Alicia, it's nice to see you again. Remember me? My name is [_____] and this is [_____]. When we came out to your house a couple of weeks ago, we mentioned that we would be checking back in to see how things were going. After we met, we discussed that after-school time at home is sometimes difficult for you, and we wanted to see if we could help you get connected to some activities you'd find fun to do." This is a clear explanation of purpose that would likely help to reassure the client, who had walked into the room with hunched shoulders and a worried expression.

Example 2: An intern, whose foundation placement was at a long-term care facility, introduced herself to Ms. Howell, a 93-year-old woman who had been in the assisted living program for the last six months: "Hi, Ms. Howell, I'm [_____], the social work intern at [the long-term nursing facility]. My supervisor mentioned that you have some concerns about living here. If you'd like, I'm available to talk with you about what we can do to ease your transition and make it better for you. If that's something you're interested in, would you like to talk now or is there a better time? I'm here all day and tomorrow." The intern has made it clear that he is available and he has explained the purpose. He has also conveyed that they can work together and that she has a role in deciding what happens to her.

EXERCISES

Question 1: The intern in this case is working in a school setting where she sees children who are having behavioral management problems in the classroom. In the following dialogue, she greets her client, an eight-year-old Latino, Adam, whom she is meeting for the first time.

> **Intern:** Hello, Adam! How are you?
> **Adam:** Good.
> **Intern:** Glad to hear that. My name is [_____] and I'll be your counselor for this year.
> **Adam:** Oh.
> **Intern:** You remember working with the counselor from last year?
> **Adam:** Yeah.
> **Intern:** Just like that, I'll be working with you this year.

PICK THE CORRECT ALTERNATIVE RESPONSE THE INTERN COULD HAVE USED HERE.

A. Ask the client what he did with the counselor last year to find out what he liked about the experience (or didn't like) and to identify and correct any misperceptions.
B. Frame the duration of services around what he is able to accomplish rather than pose the time period around a length of time that the client is mandated to attend.
C. Establish more rapport in terms of "small talk."
D. A, B, and C are all correct.

Question 2: An intern wrote the following as the stated purpose of a contact with a 14-year-old client who has been exhibiting behavioral problems at home and at school: "The goal was to persuade the judge that Michael's behavior has improved enough to move him from residential care to foster care."

WHAT IS TRUE ABOUT THE WAY THE PURPOSE IS STATED?

A. The purpose is adequate as it is stated.
B. The problem with the intern's stated purpose is that it involves the actions of the judge rather than the actions of the client.

C. The purpose could be posed as to "identify what needs to happen to show the judge you are ready to move to foster care."

D. B and C

Question 3: Which of the following intern statements best describes the purpose for the contact?

A. I'm basically here to help check in and see how things are going with the students. I was hoping that we could just get together to get to know one another today. . . . (After non-verbal response by client) What brought you here?

B. (After some brief small talk) The purpose of this meeting is for us to have a conversation about your current housing situation. I will ask a lot of questions to try and figure out what housing services I may be able to provide for you as well as to try and link you with other services in the community. Lastly, once we have gathered all your information, I will add your family's name to the shelter wait list. If you have any questions or need clarification on any information I'm giving you, please feel free to stop me.

C. Hey, how are you? What's been going on?

D. I just wanted to see how you are doing today and how you are feeling.

SHORT ANSWER QUESTIONS

Scenario 1: The social work intern in this case is visiting Chantelle, an African American, 17-year-old foster youth whose two-year-old child, Raquel, lives with Chantelle's biological mother. The intern's stated purpose is a "check-in to see how things are going."

Intern: So how has your weekend been? Did you do anything fun?

Chantelle: It's been good. I went to homecoming last night.

Intern: Oh, you did? That's great! Did you take any pictures?

Chantelle: Yeah. Let me go get them.

Intern: Oh, my gosh, you look beautiful! I love your dress.

Chantelle: Thanks. It was good. Yeah, me and [foster mother] got my dress last week. And I got my nails done too.

Intern: Wow, it sounds like you had a lot of fun.

Chantelle: Yup, I did.

Intern: That's wonderful that you went. I'm glad to hear that you had a good time.

Chantelle: I'm going to go get my progress report to show you. It's not that good though. [She returns with the report.] I do have an "F" in English, but my teacher said if I turn in my assignments then she'll change the grade.

Intern: Do you know what assignments you are missing?

Chantelle: Yeah, she told me. I'm going to do them this week and then get my grade changed.

Intern: Yeah, the sooner you get those done the better. You don't want to get behind in other work while you're making up those assignments. Your other grades are good, though. That's great!

Chantelle: Yeah. And I want to talk to you about living by myself with Raquel.

Intern: Okay. So if you get custody of her, then you don't want to live here anymore?

Chantelle: Yeah. I want to see if I can live in an apartment by myself with her.

Intern: Okay, well we can talk about that option, but until the court determines who has custody, we can't really realistically look into that. But I think that's great that you are voicing your needs/wants, and if that is a realistic goal, in the future we can work toward that.

Chantelle: I mean, I like living here and all, but there are a lot of people.

Intern: So living here makes you feel a little crowded, and you want more privacy. I can understand that.

Chantelle: Yeah.

Intern: One thing you should think about if you do want to live independently is child care. Have you thought at all about that? Who would watch her when you are in school and at work?

Chantelle: Yeah. I want to see if I can switch her day care to the day care that I work at. I think my mom gets a voucher, so I want to switch that to where I am.

Intern: To be honest, I really don't know how the vouchers work or if it is possible to switch her to your child care. That is something I can look into for you.

Chantelle: Okay.

Intern: Is there anything else you want to talk to me about?

Chantelle: No. I mainly just wanted to tell you about Raquel and wanting to live with her alone.

Intern: Your advocating for your needs is a great step toward gaining your independence. We can discuss living with her independently, but we will need to look into what is best for both you and her. And don't forget to complete your assignments for English. Keep up the good work in your other classes!

Chantelle: Thanks.

Question: What do you think of the stated purpose of this contact?

Scenario 2: Keisha is an 18-year-old, female, African American foster child, and the oldest of eight siblings divided among three foster homes. The intern is one of a long line of "helpers" with whom the client has worked. She is frustrated that she still has to have case management when all but one of her siblings have been adopted recently and are not required to have further services. The intern's stated purpose of the contact is to "engage with her and help make the most of a required relationship." Keisha says, "It's nothing personal. I just don't feel like I need case management, and all of these meetings anymore. I mean, I'm 18 and I work very hard … all the time really. I'm doing well in school and at home, and I just don't feel like these extra meetings do anything other than add another meeting to my already stressful day."

Question: What is your assessment of the stated purpose of the work?

Scenario 3: Maria is a 32-year-old single Latina with an 18-month-old son. Child protective services (CPS) has an ongoing case with this family because of the child's low weight and failure to thrive. Maria speaks no English and is reported to have emigrated from a small village in Guatemala two years ago. Since CPS has been involved, the child has gained weight but is still only at the third percentile. In a process recording, the intern stated that the purpose of the contact was to gather Maria's social information in order to better understand her family support and her motives for being in this country. The intern described the meeting in the following way: "Maria was a little defensive and guarded at the beginning of the meeting, asking me why I was asking questions and who else would be reading what I was writing down. After letting her know that I was asking her questions about her history because I wanted to get to know her better, and assuring her that everything that she was telling me was confidential and would be seen by only my supervisor and me, she seemed to relax a bit."

Question: What is your assessment of the stated purpose of the session?

In this chapter I devote a lot of attention to defining a purpose, both for ongoing work and for individual contacts with clients, because this is often where students flounder, to the detriment of their clients. If the purpose is not fully developed, the rest of the work may be aimless, may lack professionalism, and could actually victimize clients by subjecting them to services without any particular purpose. We can't assume that our very presence is helpful to clients without a purpose for it. The development of a relationship can be part of a therapeutic process, but I believe that the purpose of contact is a basic cornerstone. The clients we generally see at the foundation level are suffering from serious problems that often can be ameliorated only through implementation of concrete services. Further, because of the nature of their position, interns offer time-limited services for one or two semesters. This means that the work they provide has to be focused in nature.

A problem related to having a lack of purpose is the duplication of another professional's purpose. Some clients seem inundated with contacts from various professionals whose work is overlapping. Social workers usually perform under scarce resources; when there is duplication of services, resources are not being used efficiently. When you suspect such duplication, you should talk to your supervisor about its occurrence and discuss how your time at the internship can be used more effectively. You can also involve your faculty liaison if this conversation does not change the way services are delivered.

EXERCISES FOR YOUR PRACTICE

1: To end this section, write down an introduction of yourself, your role, and the purpose of your work/contact with a client to demonstrate that you understand how to create a contact that has purpose.

2: **Program planning question:** What other services are being provided to the client? Is there any duplication that will be provided by your work? If so, how do you plan to handle that? Write down who you would speak to. What will you say?

MEETING WITH FAMILIES

Along with addressing parents first, their concerns should also be heard first, respecting their position in the family as the people in charge. However, children should also be allowed to voice their opinions and concerns. Indeed, each person in the family should be given a turn to speak. In families where there are raised voices, or where there is interrupting and arguing, you can set down ground rules, such as "I would like to hear from everyone, so each person in the family needs a chance to speak. Even if you disagree with what another person is saying, I'd appreciate your listening to his or her position. You will get a chance to give your side as well."

There are certain situations in which you would not work with a family together. These include:

1. if you are concerned that there may be child abuse. You would not want the child to be silenced by her family or punished for what she has said.
2. if a parent is being emotionally abusive to a child when the parent is referring to the child (i.e., calling them "lazy," "hateful," "bad," "just like so and so…"), and your efforts to curtail this behavior have gone ignored.

   A way to curtail this behavior is to reframe some of the parents' statements so they are personalized: "You're very frustrated because it seems to you like your child doesn't listen, and you feel helpless about your influence over his behavior." In this statement, I try to validate the feelings of frustration and provide a positive intention, while also limiting the behavior. If a parent persists, I will ask the child to leave the room so that parents can express themselves freely, but I will make it clear that they must limit this conversation in front of the child. Instead, I encourage them to focus on the behaviors of the child rather than references to the child's character. "What would you like to see her doing instead?" This wording places focus on the child's *behavior*, not on the child herself.
3. if the parent is talking about matters that are inappropriate around a child, such as his or her own sexual behavior. You should separate the child and address with the parent that this is a matter better discussed only with an adult, not in front of a child. If parents insist that the child doesn't listen or hear, you can make mention of the fact that children are often taking in more than they appear to be.

HOME VISITING

Social work has a long history of home visiting, and in many settings, services are provided in the home. There are many advantages to home-based services. Logistically speaking, the limitations of clients who don't have transportation, issues of immobility in disabled clients, as well as child care problems can be eliminated by going to the client's home. The social worker can view the client in his or her natural environment, which gives a more accurate picture of what his or her life is like. It helps the social worker identify challenges that must be overcome in terms of basic needs or safety. The social worker also meets other people who might be living with the client, assessing their level of support and engaging them as needed in services to assist the client. When social workers introduce clients to new behaviors, they can practice with the client in the setting where the new behaviors may actually be used, thereby improving generalizability.

For all the positives, however, there are also potential problems with home visiting. Foremost is the lack of structure and boundaries that exist in an office setting. How long should you stay? When other people are in the home, should they be included or should you try to seek privacy for the client? What about distractions, such as the TV, children playing, the telephone ringing, and so forth? How do you politely ensure that these distractions do not get in the way of the work?

DISTRACTIONS

Let's start with distractions. Often, a television will be playing when you enter the home. One thing that has worked well for me is to say to clients, "Do you mind if we turn that off? I get easily distracted, and I want to be able to focus on you." Although clients have seemed surprised by this request, in every instance they have agreed. After all, how they can argue with the fact that it is about my distraction and my wanting to help them? If we allow the television (or radio) to stay on, the message we're conveying is that these are not professional services, that the client does not have to provide his or her undivided attention, and that the work we're doing together is not important.

THE PRESENCE OF MULTIPLE PEOPLE

Another problem with home visiting is that a number of people may be at the home for a variety of reasons—overcrowded living conditions, a chaotic family life, the desire of clients to be protected from the social worker by surrounding themselves with people who are not involved in their case. I have already talked about making introductions, which can include anyone who is present in the home. If the information is not supplied, you can ask about the person's relationship to the client and mention the private nature of the ensuing discussion.

When I worked as a therapist for a community-based juvenile offender monitoring program, a 13-year-old boy had confessed that his mother often hit him (Corcoran & Franklin, 1998). I had not met the mother, but in order to intervene, I received permission from the boy to talk to her. When I arrived at her house, two men were at the kitchen table with her. I mentioned that what we were talking about would be private and that it would be better if we talked alone. She told the men to leave, and they did. It wasn't clear who the men were and why they were there, but I suspect that she did not want to have the conversation she knew was coming and wanted to have "backup" to stop it from happening. When clients show this kind of resistance, one must politely address the barriers the client may have put into place. It is important when meeting with clients to have a private, quiet place. Sometimes this may mean meeting in another room or even outside. I often met with my teenage clients from a juvenile justice program on their front steps or another place outside if the inside was overcrowded or noisy.

STRUCTURE AND BOUNDARIES

Another potential problem with home visiting is the lack of structure and boundaries, which can lead the client to see the roles as more social than professional. It's easy for the social worker to fall prey to this as well. A time limit and a clear purpose help to maintain structure in the visit. In some settings, home-based services are provided for a required number of hours per week. One problem with this arrangement is that it ignores the fact that goals and progress should be based on the way services are structured rather than time itself. This could actually encourage the client and the social worker to just "hang out," filling in the required time. For those motivated to change, it does not reward positive movement toward goals, because the social worker will continue to be there whether or not the client is working.

SAFETY AND SANITARY CONDITIONS

Other issues that arise in making home visits involve, depending on the setting, the sanitary conditions and the safety of the home. When working with child welfare, I visited homes in which large cockroaches were plainly visible. An extreme example involved one of my fellow interns at our foundation field placement opening a cabinet at a client's home, spilling a flood of cockroaches into her shirt. In instances like these, the sanitary and safety conditions will be the first goal to work on with clients, helping them to figure out how they will organize and clean, as well as providing necessary advocacy (assisting the client or contacting the apartment manager about spraying for pests or fixing unsafe appliances or electrical wiring).

I have not personally encountered any violations or threats to my safety, although I often made home visits alone into housing projects. I recognize that these may happen, but they are rare. Following common sense precautions is important: Tell your office where you are going and what time you are expected back; keep a door visible and accessible in case you need to leave. If you feel like your safety is being threatened, leave the home. Always carry your mobile phone.

FOOD AND DRINKS

Another issue with home visiting and its social nature is that you may be offered food and/or drink by your clients. It is a generally accepted practice that social workers do not eat or drink with clients. In some cultures, however, turning down an offer of food or drink is considered rude, so how can we be culturally sensitive and still maintain professional boundaries? There are a variety of ways that this can be handled. I have known social workers who always bring a beverage with them to home visits so that they can claim their own. Others make excuses, such as "No, thank you, I just ate" or "I'm trying to lose weight." Some people have told me that in order to not appear rude, they have taken a pastry or some other similar offering "to go" to eat later. Others have mentioned that in certain situations, they would not take offered beverages because there have been no clean cups or glasses.

In your setting, do you make home visits?
If yes:

1. How is the contact structured?
2. If the contact has a specific time requirement, how do you ensure that the work is geared toward goals and progress on them rather than the time allotted?
3. How do you handle distractions that arise in the home?
4. How do you ensure your safety?
5. What are the sanitary and safety conditions of the home? If they are poor, how do you help the client address these?
6. How do you handle offers of food and/or drink?

CONCLUSION

The purpose of this chapter has been to give you some tools that will help you feel more comfortable and confident as you begin your contacts with clients. Some other situations that beginning helpers find awkward are when clients do not talk or answer with one-word response, or the opposite problem, when clients are loquacious to the point of losing focus. We leave you with two other exhibits that address these types of situations (Exhibits 1.1 and 1.2).

EXHIBIT 1.1: **What do I do now? My client keeps going off on unrelated tangents!**

For initial instances of getting off track:
1. Interrupt politely ("I'm sorry to interrupt, but . . .") and redirect ". . . we have only 45 minutes, and I know it's important for you to get back custody of your children, so I want to make sure that we focus on what needs to be done so this can happen."
2. Reflect underlying feelings and concerns ("You're still very angry about having to come here . . .").
3. Ensure that you are starting where the client is ("I came to talk to you about options for employment today, but it sounds like your health is more pressing. Shall we talk about that instead?").

Options for recurring instances:
1. Make a general observation about this tendency.
   Example: "I notice that it's hard for you to stay with what we're talking about today. What's going on?"
2. Make an observation if you see a particular pattern.
   Example: "I notice that when we start discussing your relationship with your husband, you have a difficult time staying with that and you bring up a lot of other topics."
3. Inquire about how this pattern may be serving them.
   Example: "How is it helpful to talk about all these other topics when we try to work on parenting?"

EXHIBIT 1.2: **What do I do now? My client doesn't talk!**

---

1. Allow silence (up to 30 seconds).
2. Rephrase the question.
3. Ask a relationship question.
4. Say, "I know you don't know, so just make it up."

We work with clients and their families most effectively when there is a clear reason for each meeting and when we collaborate on accomplishing our purpose. Due to the nature of the helping relationship, it is important to remember that our relationships with clients are professional in nature, not social. This is particularly important to keep in mind when we are in the client's home.

CHAPTER 2

ENGAGEMENT TECHNIQUES

With Emily Brown and Bryan Norman

Engagement with the client is the first stage of the helping process. Foremost, engagement involves establishing a basis for collaborative work. In any collaborative relationship with a client, the social worker must convey concern, empathy, respect, and acceptance of the individual. This is the case even when a worker does not agree with or condone the previous behaviors of the client (DePanfilis, 2000) and/or when the client is nonvoluntary to the change process. Along with building a collaborative relationship, recognizing and eliciting strengths in the client and orienting the client toward goals and change are also tasks of engagement. This chapter introduces techniques, most of which are drawn from solution-focused therapy, that will help operationalize some of these concepts.

ALIGN WITH CLIENT'S PERSPECTIVE AND POSITION

Often, as social workers, we enter into work with clients believing we know what they should do to improve their lives; as a result, we may be tempted to believe that it is our job to convince them of this. But if we hold one perspective and the client is in a completely different position, we risk becoming polarized, and the client is likely to become defensive and even more entrenched in a position against change (Berg, 1994). A central part of the collaboration between worker and client is that the client feels that the worker is on his or her side.

One trap practitioners fall into when they first start working with clients is to force them to admit guilt and responsibility, such as for child physical abuse (Christensen, Todahl, & Barrett, 1999), or to accept a label ("I am an alcoholic") (Miller & Rollnick, 2002), which may lead to an impasse in the process of change. Although the practitioner need not condone harmful or illegal behaviors, he or she must convey understanding of the client's situation and focus on what the client can do from this point forward to ensure that the same problem does not reoccur. People are generally more willing to work on their current behavior rather than continually discussing what has happened in the past.

I have examples of becoming polarized with clients in my first social work job as a victim services counselor for a police department. My primary task, as part of the police case, was to interview children who had been abused and then to counsel the families and make referrals, as appropriate. One of the main referrals was for ongoing psychotherapy for the children who had been sexually abused. At times, parents would reveal that they had also been sexually victimized as children. I would, on occasion, find myself becoming polarized when I would emphasize the importance of their seeking psychotherapy for this past abuse. Some parents would offer reasons why they did not need to receive therapy, such as providing evidence of their adjustment now. In hindsight, I should have instead pursued the strengths that they believed had helped them to rise above their negative pasts. In this way, I might have empowered them to better manage their extremely difficult circumstances—dealing with disclosure of sexual abuse of a child.

Another example of becoming polarized took place at the victim services unit where counselors worked with domestic violence victims. We often tried to convince the victims to leave their partners, offering various arguments as to why they should do so. However, this stance put us at odds with our clients, as they would offer alternative arguments for why they could not leave. A woman who is a victim of abuse has already been disempowered by her partner; she does not need to be further disempowered by a counselor telling her what she must do.

It may seem difficult to conceptualize how to align with nonvoluntary clients who have committed child abuse or domestic violence, or have severe drug and alcohol problems. One specific way to do this is to side with the client against an external entity, as in, "I wonder what we need to do to convince my supervisor so that she can close your case." An example of this was enacted in a group intervention at a drug court setting. One of the women mandated to attend the group said, "I don't belong here. I don't know why I have to come. It's useless." The group leader responded, "I wonder what we can get done in this group so we can tell your probation officer you got a lot out of this." This question, although collaborative in nature, also places the responsibility for change on the client, so that you do not have to talk them into change or otherwise convince them of its necessity.

ORIENTATION TOWARD GOALS

From the initial contact with clients, you can begin to orient them to the goals that need to be achieved. With voluntary clients you can ask definitive-language questions:

- "How can I be helpful so that you will know coming here was a good idea?"
- "What will your life look like when our work has been successful?"
- "What would you like to get out of talking to me today?"

In the introduction, mention was made about using language to imply change; note that the previous questions indicate that change will occur and, hence, the language offers a hopeful perspective. These types of questions also indicate another key element of collaboration; the client is an active agent in the change process. Relatedly, the questions give the client internal agency over the problem—and solution—rather than the more externally based, standard opening questions, such as "What brings you here today?" (Greene, Lee, Trask, & Rheinscheld, 2005). (More on the construction of solution-focused questions is presented in Chapter 3).

The following example shows how a social work intern at a faith-based assistance agency helped Charles, a 20-year-old African American man, formulate a goal in her opening contact with him.

Intern: What made you decide to come here for help?

Charles: I saw. . . so that I'm not just spending without thinking about it.

Intern: So the sign in the lobby that said you might be able to get help with how to manage the money you make—you would like to be more financially savvy. What will your life look like when we've finished working on that together?

Charles: Hopefully I will have a savings account set up and a better way of managing my finances so I know where my money is going and where I need to possibly cut back.

Intern: It seems like you are worried that you are spending your money on unnecessary things and you want to have a little more control to start saving money.

While Charles in the example above came for help voluntarily, nonvoluntary clients also respond well to goal orientation from the start, since they are often motivated to complete their services as quickly as possible. With mandated clients, you can ask them about the referral source: "Whose idea was it that you come here today?" You can then proceed to inquire about what the client must accomplish; for example, "What does [the judge] need to see to know that you don't have to come here anymore?" With this type of questioning, it is the client who articulates the changes to be made, not the worker. This approach respects the client's ability to understand what needs to happen and helps the client internalize the goal by saying it out loud.

Some people come for help initially motivated to make changes, but then become interested only in another person making changes rather than themselves. This is most evident in romantic partnerships (they want their partners to act differently) and with parents who want their children to improve their behavior. Usually, such clients will want to talk about what they don't want: "I don't want him to yell and curse." Your job will be to help the person identify the positive behavior(s) that needs to replace the negative behavior: "What would you like to see him doing instead?" Generally, people have a difficult time answering this question because they have been so focused on problem behavior. In order to probe for behavioral indicators, you can ask, "If I was taping her through a video camera, what would I see her doing when she is acting the way you want her to act?" This type of question places responsibility on the client to be clear and concrete about what he or she wants from the other person. You can further empower the person to be a more active participant in the change process when you ask, "What will *you* be doing when she is acting the way you want?" This question implies the circular nature of interaction patterns. When one person is doing something differently, the other person is forced to change his or her part in the interaction as well.

SOLUTION-FOCUSED ENGAGEMENT TECHNIQUES

Exhibit 2.1 summarizes techniques that are helpful for joining with nonvoluntary clients. Exhibit 2.2 lists those techniques that can be used with clients who want another person to change, and Exhibit 2.3 is specific to those cases where you are trying to engage parents in change strategies for their children. Many of these techniques are elaborated in the section below.

COMPLIMENTS

Clients may feel defensive when they first see a practitioner, expecting to be judged and criticized. By complimenting them on any strengths and resources you see or that they

---

EXHIBIT 2.1: **Strategies for Engaging Nonvoluntary Clients**

1. *Orient the client toward meeting the requirements of the mandate*: "Whose idea was it that you come here? What does _____ need to see happen to say that you don't have to come here anymore?"
2. *Ask clients to view themselves from the perspective of another person*: "What would (your probation officer, partner, parent) say needs to happen so that our time has been worthwhile?
3. *Side with the client against an external entity*: "What will we need to do to convince _____ that you no longer need to come here?"
4. *Have the client identify a goal in which he or she is interested*: "What is something you would like to accomplish in our time together?"

EXHIBIT 2.2: **Engagement Strategies for Those Interested in Change by Another Person**

1. *Coping questions*: "What resources have you drawn upon to cope with the situation?"
2. *Normalizing*: De-pathologizing clients' concerns as normal life challenges. "This often happens in marriages after the birth of a baby."
3. *Reframing*: Introducing the positive elements of a behavior initially viewed as negative. "The fact that you are arguing so much shows that you care very much about this relationship and would like it to be better."
4. *Orienting clients toward what they want to see rather than their complaints*: "What would you like (your child, your parent, your partner) to be doing instead of (complaint)?" "Rather than interrupting, what will your child be doing when he wants your attention?"
5. *Emphasizing the circular nature of interaction patterns*: "What will you be doing when your child is behaving/your partner is talking to you more/your teacher is helping?" "When your wife leaves the dishes rather than nagging you to do them right away, what will you do?"

---

1. Emphasize the dominant role that the parent plays in the child's role, and downplay your own importance: "You are the most important person to your child, more than I ever would be in my hour a week I see her. If I work with you, you can be much more effective than I could ever hope to be."
2. Explain children's cognitive limitations: "Young children have a difficult time learning a new behavior in one setting, such as my office, and then generalizing that skill to another context. When you learn what I will be teaching him, you can prompt him for these behaviors at home and then reinforce him for doing them."
3. Explain the limitation of children's attention: "Children (even ones who can listen and follow directions) will be able to focus on only one subject, especially if the subject is an uncomfortable one, for a short time."
4. Mention research showing that training parents to change behavior in their children is more effective for young children with conduct problems (up to age 12) than is working with the children individually using cognitive behavior therapy (McCart, Priester, Davies, & Azen, 2006). Some tentative evidence even suggests that working only with the parents is more effective than working with both the parents and the child (Lundahl et al., 2006).
5. Consider the NASW Code of Ethics mandate that "Social workers understand that relationships between and among people are an important vehicle for change. Social workers engage people as partners in the helping process. Social workers seek to strengthen relationships among people in a purposeful effort to promote, restore, maintain, and enhance the well-being of individuals, families, social groups, organizations, and communities." This ethic demands that we engage parents as partners in the helping process with the recognition that the relationship between parent and child is an important vehicle for change.

demonstrate, you can enhance their cooperation and limit their defensiveness (Greene, Lee, Trask, & Rheinscheld, 2005). An example of complimenting is presented in the case of the adult caregiver Beth, who struggles with her mother's behaviors that are exacerbated by her diagnosis of dementia. Beth relates that when she is very frustrated, "I refuse to talk to her anymore, and I make Perry deal with her instead. Then, when he gets fed up with her we take the phone off the hook. If we are out somewhere and she annoys us so much that we can't handle it, we bring her back here to the retirement community." Beth may feel defensive and/or guilty as she describes the situation, but the intern surprises her by offering a compliment: "It's good that you can recognize when the caregiving gets to be too much. I'm glad that you have times of respite when your mother is at the retirement community." The intern shows her understanding of Beth's difficult situation and recognizes the strengths inherent in her statement, rather than judging her actions.

De Jong and Berg (2008) suggest a form of complimenting called "indirect complimenting" in which positive traits and behaviors are implied. Examples of indirect complimenting include "How were you able to do that?" and "How did you figure that out?"

These questions push clients to become aware of the resources they used to achieve success. When clients articulate their own strengths, it can be more empowering than when they are directly told by the practitioner.

EXERCISES

Exercise 1: In this scenario, the social work intern conducted an intake with an 18-year-old female who had left college due to depression. What could you find to compliment in this exchange? What specifically would you say?

Intern: So what's going on?
Laura: Well, I just left college because I was feeling really depressed and was having suicidal thoughts.
Intern: How long was this going on?
Laura: It started when I got to school and had to go to the hospital down there a few weeks ago.
Intern: What hospital were you going to and how long did you stay?
Laura: I was going to [_____]. I was there for three days.
Intern: Oh, okay. Are you currently having these suicidal thoughts?
Laura: No.
Intern: How severe were these thoughts? Did you have a plan or ever attempt?
Laura: No, I never attempted or had a plan. I was just feeling like I didn't care.
Intern: So you were feeling hopeless?
Laura: Yeah.
Intern: Can you tell me about some of your symptoms?
Laura: I've just been really down and depressed. I haven't been able to do much.
Intern: Have you been able to sleep?
Laura: Yeah.
Intern: What about your appetite? How has that been?
Laura: I haven't been able to eat much.
Intern: Have you lost or gained any weight?
Laura: Yeah I've lost about 15 pounds since I was in the hospital.
Intern: Oh, wow. That's a lot. Do you have any substance-abuse issues?
Laura: No.
Intern: Do you have any family history of mental illnesses?
Laura: No.
Intern: Ok. What medications are you on?
Laura: [_____].
Intern: How many milligrams?
Laura: 60.
Intern: Okay. How long have you been on them?
Laura: About three weeks.
Intern: Have they been working?
Laura: Not really.

Exercise 2: Sara is a 17-year-old adolescent and mother of two-year-old Maggie. She has a history of truancy and is enrolled in ninth grade at an alternative school. Sara currently lives with her mother, Rachelle. In the following scenario, discuss how the intern could use the technique of complimenting:

Intern: How have things been since I was here last week?

Rachelle: Bad. Sara left Maggie here on Friday and didn't tell anyone where she was going. She didn't come back until late and then she left again at 10 a.m. on Saturday and didn't come home until 5 p.m. last night. She said she was going to the store. It doesn't take you that long to go to the store.

Intern: She didn't tell anyone where she was going?

Rachelle: No. We all tried calling her but she didn't pick up her phone, didn't answer texts. She doesn't follow the rules. She doesn't listen. Sara does what Sara wants to do.

Intern: It seems like she doesn't listen to you at all. What would you want your relationship with her to be?

Rachelle: Perfect.

Intern: Explain what you mean by perfect.

Rachelle: When she doesn't lie. Answer her phone when we call her. She says I don't know how to talk to her. She does what she wants. She wants to be a mother, but how can she? I told her she needs to read the Bible or something.

Intern: So you want a relationship where she communicates with you more. Do you do things as a family?

Rachelle: Oh yeah, but she doesn't ever participate. We go to the movies, bowling, and laser tag.

Intern: It sounds like you do a lot of activities together. Why doesn't Sara ever participate?

Rachelle: Because she's never around and she has such a bad attitude that nobody wants her to come 'cause she'll ruin the mood.

Intern: So everyone else does things together, but Sara is left out?

Rachelle: Yeah, 'cause she doesn't want to participate.

Intern: Is there ever a time that she will participate? Tell me about those times.

Rachelle: We just talk. Joke around. We won't yell at each other, just be normal.

Intern: Why do you think that doesn't happen often?

Rachelle: Because she has an attitude problem. She's nice when she wants to be.

Intern: She acknowledges the fact that she has an attitude.

Rachelle: She doesn't care. A while ago she got a ride from her sister and stole money out of the glove compartment. My older daughter knew how much money was in there. She had no reason to lie.

Intern: Do you know why she would be stealing?

Rachelle: I try to buy her things to make her happy, but it's never good enough. She's just disrespectful.

REFRAMING

Akin to complimenting is the technique of reframing. Through reframing, the practitioner introduces people to a new way of viewing the problem. In other words, the client is given credit for positive aspects of his or her behavior (Berg, 1994) or his or her motives are cast in a benevolent light (Morris, Alexander, & Waldron, 1988). Through reframing, individuals are introduced to a novel way of viewing some aspect of themselves, others, or their problem or situation. A new perspective on the problem can generate new actions in accordance with this different frame of reference (Bertolino & O'Hanlon, 2002).

An example of reframing can be offered with Beth, the adult caregiver who struggles to manage her elderly mother's dementia. The intern's reframe went as follows: "Caregiving can be very overwhelming, but your coming in to discuss her behavior today shows what dedicated caregivers you are for your mother."

NORMALIZING

Normalizing involves de-pathologizing clients' concerns as normal life challenges. For instance, if an individual grieves the loss of a loved one and feels that she is "going crazy" because she hasn't "snapped out of it," information about the length of the grieving process and the phases that are common may reassure her that her reactions and concerns are typical of those who are going through the same process or life event.

To look at normalizing, we again look to the scenario with the adult caregiver, Beth. The intern stated, "The annoyance that you feel toward your mother is normal. It can be difficult trying to understand why your mother is acting the way that she is." This normalizing statement acts to allay Beth's agitation about her mother's behavior and to lessen the guilt over her response to it.

Another example of normalizing involves a 29-year-old client from Latin America who had recently given birth and was referred to the social work intern at the health clinic for symptoms of depression. The client said, "I've been feeling sad. I cry for no reason. Our financial situation is really hard at the moment. It makes me really sad to see that we don't have enough food for our children. I don't care if I don't eat, but my children need food." The following statement could normalize the impact of her suffering from the multiple stressors she faces: "You've just had a baby, which is in itself a very stressful experience, and your hormones may still be in flux. You're having financial problems, and you are worried about your children getting enough to eat. Most people dealing with all that at once would be having a difficult time. So it's no wonder you are feeling sad and overwhelmed."

Normalizing also works with the "negative spiral" that sometimes occurs with problems. Some people become so concerned with the problem that they escalate to greater proportions. A common example involves parents who center on their adolescent's style of dress as a source of contention, and frequent arguments about this topic ensue, causing the relationship to deteriorate. Experimentation with style and other aspects of identity can be normalized as typical adolescent stage behavior. By de-pathologizing the concerns, the original problem is kept in proportion to its nature.

Exercise: Review again the scenario of Laura, the 18-year-old woman who left college due to her depression. How could you use the technique of *normalizing* in this situation?

EXERCISE FOR YOUR PRACTICE

Create a normalizing statement that you could use with a client you are currently seeing or one that would fit a hypothetical situation that could occur at your agency setting.

COPING QUESTIONS

Coping questions from solution-focused therapy are also useful for engagement. As a function of seeing clients who are impoverished, social workers often hear about past and current difficulties that seem unmanageable. Coping questions not only validate the extent to which people have struggled, they also ask clients to reflect upon the resources they have used to manage their struggles. Types of coping questions include the following (Bertolino & O'Hanlon, 2002):

- "How have you coped with the problem?"
- "How do you manage? How do you have the strength to go on?"

- "This has been a very difficult problem for you. How have you managed to keep things from getting even worse?"
- "How have you managed to keep your sanity and hope in the midst of these problems?"
- "What qualities do you possess that you are able to tap into in times of trouble?"
- "What is it about you that allows you to keep going?"
- "What would others say are the qualities that keep you going?"
- "In the midst of what has happened, how have you managed to keep going?"
- "What percentage of the time are you dealing with this? How do you cope during this time? What makes it a little better the other percentage of the time?"
- "What do you tell yourself to keep going? What do you say to yourself to keep your sanity and hope when things are really hard?"

A social work intern placed in a hospice care setting worked with a 57-year-old man, Howard, whose wife had died five months prior. He struggled with depression and although he said he wouldn't harm himself, he found the pain of his loss so unbearable that suicide entered his mind as a way to end the pain. When the intern asked him a coping question, he said that reading about grief, attending a support group, and helping others through their own grief (a coworker who had lost his father and a fellow group member whose husband had died) all helped him cope with the pain. Howard explained that during these times, he is not so focused on how difficult things have been for himself. When asked, "What would others say keeps you going?" Howard answered that his need to honor his wife's memory, the presence of his son in his life, and the support of his coworkers are things that others would say. The intern also asked, "What do you say to yourself to keep your sanity and hope when things are really hard?" He replied, "I just focus on how strong my wife was through her illness. She just kept fighting. I don't want to let her down now."

Another example of using coping questions to bring out strengths is shown in the following scenario:

Sean is an 18-year-old Caucasian, gay male who is dealing with being cut off emotionally from his parents when they discovered his sexual orientation. He was unemployed and homeless until recently and is now seeking case management through the homeless and low-income drop-in program, where he comes for some of his meals.

Intern: Sean, what would you like to see as a result of our talking today?
Sean: Well, as you know I was homeless for about a year after my parents kicked me out of their house when they found out I am gay. Things are going so much better now. I have a job, I support myself, and I have an apartment. But I just don't like myself. I think there's something wrong with me.
Intern: How does this relate to your coming out about being gay?
Sean: (teary) I know it's been a year, but I still can't believe all that's happened. I haven't heard a word from my parents, not a call or text. And my birthday was two weeks ago. I was alone.
Intern: Sean, it must hurt so much being rejected by your parents. How have you been able to deal with this over the past year?

Sean: I did what I had to do.

Intern: I have to say, though, that from what I've heard of your story, you are a very resourceful person. Not many 18-year-olds could have been able to do what you did. In fact, even many homeless adults find it very hard to get back on their feet again, yet you found a job and an apartment. How did you do it?

Sean: I forced myself to keep going. There were days where I wanted to give up. I would break down and cry, and I would get so angry at my folks. I honestly think it was that anger that pushed me to keep going. I would just say to myself, "Sean, you are on your own now. Do you want them to see you fail? Hell no! I will show them. I'm going to get my life together and I'm going to be okay without them."

Intern: So, the anger that you felt, that you feel, was channelled into. . . kind of like a mantra that kept pushing you forward. That's remarkable, Sean.

Sean: It didn't feel so remarkable at the time. I just did what I needed to do to be okay.

Intern: In addition to your determination, what other things have you done to help you cope with everything you have been facing over the past year?

Sean: Well, I do have three very close friends who know I'm gay, and they hang with me no matter what. We've been friends for years. But they live about 30 minutes away, so I don't see them as much as I want to. We text a lot, though. And I have a really cool aunt. She lives on the other side of the country, but we text a lot too, and that helps.

Intern: So, staying connected has been an important way for you to get through all of this.

Sean: Definitely. I couldn't have done it all without them. Sometimes I just needed to hear that someone cared about me, and that kept me going.

Exercise: How can you use a coping question in the following scenario? What might happen as a result of using such a technique?

Mrs. Hall is a 33-year-old African American single parent with three children, ages 15, 11, and 7. She had been receiving TANF (Temporary Assistance for Needy Families) assistance for the past three years, since her husband deserted her. The intern's stated purpose for their meeting is "to help motivate her to get a job."

Intern: What would you like to see yourself doing 10 years from now?

Mrs. Hall: I haven't given it much thought.

Intern: What about your current situation; how satisfied are you with it?

Mrs. Hall: I am not satisfied about my life now; it is very difficult to live on this inadequate TANF budget, to raise three children all by myself, and to handle all the stress that comes from my husband deserting us.

Intern: I understand your concerns. While it's true that past events in your life led to your current situation, your present and future will depend largely on you.

Mrs. Hall: How do you mean?

Intern: Take your financial situation, for example. You have a choice between staying at home and seeking a job. If you don't begin learning an employable skill now, and gradually working your way up in the job, what's going to happen in about 10 years when you will no longer be eligible for the TANF payments?

Mrs. Hall: It would be nice to get a job, but there are also many reasons why it wouldn't be possible for me to get a job.

Intern: Tell me more about that.

Mrs. Hall: Eventually if I work, it would not add to my total income, because my TANF check will be reduced. I tried finding a job several times in the past and was not able to obtain one. Also, I would not be able to work and take care of my home and family.

Intern: Trying in the past and failing doesn't mean you can't be successful this time. I hope you've heard the saying "if at first you don't succeed, try again." I would encourage you to try again.

EXERCISE FOR YOUR PRACTICE

Create a coping statement that you could use with a client you are currently seeing or one that would fit a hypothetical situation that could occur at your agency setting.

ASKING CLIENTS TO SPEAK FROM THE PERSPECTIVE OF ANOTHER: RELATIONSHIP QUESTIONS

A technique from solution-focused therapy is to pose relationship questions, which get clients to view themselves from the perspective of another (de Jong & Berg, 2008). When people are in the midst of a problem, it is often difficult for them to see alternatives. By viewing the problem from another person's point of view ("What would your partner say needs to happen in our work together to know that our time has been successful?"), they can sometimes see other possibilities. Relationship questions are a useful technique for direct practice because a core value in social work is the importance of relationships. Relationship questions emphasize that we exist in relation to others and that our behavior affects and is influenced by this interpersonal context.

Relationship questions are also useful when people respond with "I don't know" to your questions. They help relieve people of having to come up with the answers when they may feel pressured or stuck. By taking the perspective of another person, people are also empowered to view themselves more realistically. When I worked with teenagers in the juvenile justice system, I found that they often presented themselves as doing well, but when asked to view themselves from the perspective of their probation officer, teacher, or parent, they were able to more clearly see the areas where they needed to exert additional effort. Another effective use of this strategy is when working with people suffering from depression. They often have feelings of low self-worth and lack self-confidence. However, when asked to view themselves from the perspective of an employer, coworker, close friend, or family member, they often present themselves in a more favorable light. This change in viewpoint may lead to their having a more realistic, instead of overly negative, portrayal of themselves.

EXERCISE FOR YOUR PRACTICE

Create at least one relationship question for a client you are currently seeing or one that would fit a hypothetical situation that could occur at your agency setting. Consider the effect of asking relationship questions with this client.

QUESTIONS ABOUT PREVIOUS INTERVENTION

Some of the clients you work with as an intern may have had a long history of helpers before you. You might have taken a client's case by replacing a previous intern or another social worker or agency professional. In order to give clients credit for the work they have done with others and to put them in the expert position of knowing what's most helpful to them, Bertolino and O'Hanlon (2002) have suggested asking questions such as "What has been helpful about previous case management/other services you have received?" and "What has not been so helpful?" These questions help clients review their previous experiences and help them get in touch with how they have effectively used services in the past. Hearing the answers also assists practitioners in knowing what has already been tried with the client and what has worked. In that way, practitioners can steer their efforts in ways that optimally benefit their clients.

Exercise: Returning to the scenario of the 18-year-old who had left college because of her depression and suicidal thoughts, what questions would you ask regarding her previous treatment experience? What might this tell you?

Do any of your clients have a history of other services? Pose questions that would empower your client to take ownership of how he or she worked with these other services.

EXTERNALIZING

Another technique that strategically uses language is called *externalizing the problem* (White & Epston, 1990). In externalizing, a linguistic distinction is made between the presenting problem and the person; this is done by referring to the problem behavior as an external entity (the urge to drink, the invitation to argue, the anger). There are several ways to do this:

- Simply place a "the" before the term the person uses to refer to the problem (the anger, the dementia). For example, in the case of the adult caregiver, Beth, and her elderly mother, the intern refers to "the dementia," as in "What do you do when the dementia gets you really frustrated?"
- Pick up on a term the client uses to describe the problem (e.g., "nerves") and use that same label or phrase prefaced by a "the" (e.g., "the nerves").
- Depending on the client's age and preference, you can ask the client to draw a picture of the problem; in that way, the piece of artwork not only represents the externalized entity, it is concretely externalized as the artwork.
- Ask the client to give you a name: "What do you call what we've been talking about? Do you have a name for it?"

Children may select playful names, such as "sneaky poo" (for encopresis) [White & Epton, 1990], "the tornado" or "the volcano" (for anger), or "the crap" (for oppositional behaviors) [Corcoran, 2002]. In these examples, externalizing introduces a note of humor into the work.

The overall purpose of externalizing is to free the person from the belief that the problem is fixed and inherent. In this way, the oppressive nature of the problem is lifted, and more options for behavior change may be revealed. Like coping questions, externalizing allows validation of the problem while providing a bridge to discussion of solutions (Dyes & Neville, 2000). Externalizing provides a way for helpers to get on the same side as the client against the externalized entity. It provides the worker a way to talk about harmful behaviors while still demonstrating regard for the client.

After identifying the externalized entity, the next step is to empower people to fight against it by asking what are called *relative influence questions* (Bertolino & O'Hanlon, 2002, p. 133):

"What's different about the times you're able to control the _____?"
"When can you resist the urge to _____?"

"When are you able to overcome the temptation to _____?"
"What percentage of the time do you have control over _____?"
"How has _____ come between you and your _____?"
"When has _____ recruited you to do something that you later got in trouble for?"
"What intentions do you think _____ has for you?"
"When have you been able to take a stand against _____?"
"Tell me about times when _____ couldn't convince you to _____?"

Relative influence questions allow people to explore how they have struggled to overcome their problems and to understand how they can be empowered to fight against their problems, rather than viewing them as entrenched within them. The social worker, the client (and others in the client's life) can struggle collaboratively against the externalized problem; everyone is on the same side (against the problem), not mad at the client for having the problem. In this way, externalizing can reduce defensiveness.

Note in the following scenario how a 12-year-old African American boy living in foster care handles discussion about his "hoarding." The intern describes that he has been taking food from the kitchen where he lives with his foster parents—food that is meant for their in-home day care.

Intern: I heard that you decided that you didn't want a food drawer, and I was wondering if you had come up with other ways of controlling what you eat?
Damien: I just made up my mind that I am not going to do it anymore.
Intern: There is a reason that you did it before, and if you don't work through it, then it may come up again.
Damien: I don't know; I don't really understand why it was a big deal.
Intern: It was a big deal because it meant sneaking food behind your foster family's back, and you were leaving old food lying around your room. Do you think those are acceptable behaviors?
Damien: No, but I don't know why everyone is making such a big deal about it.

The child, in this case, seems to feel defensive about his behavior ("I don't really understand why it was a big deal"), and in certain ways the intern has contributed to this stance. Instead, the problem could be referred to as "the hoarding" or she could ask him to give it a name ("what do you call it when you think about it?"). Relative influence questions could follow: "When is it easier to get a handle on the hoarding?" "When can you stand up to the hoarding?"

A final advantage of externalizing is that it can incorporate cultural experiences of emotional and mental suffering, such as "the devil," "the spirits," and "the evil eye." Rather than being dismissive of people's expressions, instead their language is used and cultural explanations are cast as external entities. Then the influence of these phenomena can be explored: "When is the spell more powerful?" or "When are you able to get past the power of the spell?" or "What needs to happen to get rid of the spell?"

EXERCISES

The purpose of externalizing is to make sure that people take responsibility for their problems.

True or False [circle one]

MULTIPLE-CHOICE QUESTIONS

1. Externalizing would be used in all of the following instances EXCEPT
    A. when a person talks about having an anger problem.
    B. when a person talks about feeling depressed.
    C. when a person talks about endless arguing with a partner.
    D. when a worker gives a client a referral to a community agency.
2. All of the following are solution-focused engagement techniques EXCEPT
    A. normalizing.
    B. coping questions.
    C. decisional balance.
    D. reframing.
3. If clients ask a personal question, all of the following are optimal ways to handle this EXCEPT
    A. simply answer the question.
    B. reflect the underlying concern.
    C. ask how it might be helpful to know the information.
    D. tell the client that you would like him or her to tell you when it seems you don't understand and explain to you what he or she is going through.
4. If a client keeps responding, "I don't know," the following are all ways to handle this EXCEPT
    A. allow silence after you make a statement/ask a question.
    B. rephrase the question.
    C. ask a totally different question.
    D. say, "I know you don't know, so just make it up."
5. All of the following are part of engagement EXCEPT
    A. building rapport.
    B. telling the client what resources can be used to solve his or her problem.
    C. building a collaborative relationship.
    D. introducing yourself, your role, and the purpose of the work together.

6. Name the technique the intern is using in the second statement of the following scenario.

The client is at a residential living facility for women who have been released from prison.

Resident: Yeah, I'm just worried that since I've been in jail, they won't want me or I'm too old. Like there might be a lot of younger people going for the same job and they know all of the new technology and I won't.

Intern: So you're worried that you might not do as well as some of the younger workers.

Resident: Yeah, cause I haven't been in the field in awhile.

Intern: So you're seeing your age as a problem, but the way I see it, your age can be a positive because you have years of experience that the others won't have.

Resident: Huh, I never thought about it like that. Yeah, I guess I'm not worried about the other employees. It's more the interview.

   A. Normalizing
   B. Coping questions
   C. Decisional balance
   D. Reframing

Questions 7 and 8 involve the following scenario: The client is a 24-year-old Latina whose two-year-old was originally removed for suspected abuse and neglect. She was recently returned to her mother's home on a trial basis in an attempt to restore custody.

Social Worker: So what did you do this weekend?

Client: I'm trying to spend more time with my daughter, so I picked her up from her grandmother's to spend Saturday with her. I took her shopping.

Social Worker: How much did you spend? Remember last time when you spent $200?

Client: I just spent $150. It's okay. She needs the clothes. She's growing, and we went to the cheap stores.

Social Worker: That's a lot of money. What if you spent $100 and put $50 in the bank? Do you have a savings account, one that actually has money in it?

Client: Yes, I have two. I am going to open another one that I can use only for school, housing, or business. I want to save as much money as I can for two years.

Social Worker: That's good that you are saving money. Be careful that you don't mess up your food stamps, though.

Client: I wanted to ask you about the restraining order against C.'s father. Is there a way that we can make that permanent?

Social Worker: I don't know exactly how that works, but I can help you find out. I think it sounds like a very good idea.

Client: I also wanted to ask you about getting back custody of C.

Social Worker: I was not planning to give you back custody at the next hearing but instead the one after, in about six months.

Client: Oh (*looking down*).

Social Worker: You seem disappointed. Were you hoping you would get custody back at the next hearing?

Client: Yeah, I was just really hoping I would get her back so that this would all be over, and I would have more time to go to school or something.

Social Worker: Do you want to go back to school? I could help you find time in your schedule if you want to do that. (*G is silent.*) Well, what do you think would change if you got back custody?

Client: I would just have more time. I wouldn't have to meet with the social workers all of the time.

Social Worker: Even after you get back custody, we will still hold a protective order. You would still have to meet with me, the person in charge of your transitional housing, and the other social workers who work with you or help you with services. None of that would change.

Client: I just thought I would get custody back.

Social Worker: I just want to see that you can do everything that you have to do to keep C. You are already doing everything you need to do. You don't have to do anything new. I just want to make sure you can maintain it even after you have custody. This way I can also continue to provide you services like child care. Do you think you could start setting aside money for child care?

Client: Yes.

Social Worker: Why don't you talk to the child care providers to figure out how much it will cost. Then, starting next month, I want you to set aside money to show me that you can pay for part or all of the child care.

Client: Okay, I can start doing that for next month.

Social Worker: That would show me that you are ready and able to support yourself and C. after we return custody. I'm going to hold you to that starting next month.

7. The worker in this scenario has established a collaborative relationship.
   True or False [Circle one]

8. Considering the information that has been provided in Chapters 1 and 2, what improvements can be made?
   A. Provide a purpose to the contact.
   B. Align with the client against an external entity (e.g., the judge).
   C. Compliment the client on what she has been able to achieve so far.
   D. Meet in the office rather than the home so that the contact is more structured.
   E. A, B, and C

In the following scenario, an intern at a child welfare setting met with Sara, a 17-year-old African American teenage mother. Below, they discuss Sara's relationship with the father of her child. How would you use externalizing in this instance?

Sara: Yeah. But it's better now. We talk about things more.
Intern: So you've been working on communication with him. How so?
Sara: I don't know. We just talk about what's going on. I have an attitude problem. I would get mad about other stuff and take it out on him.
Intern: Do you think the attitude problem is the reason why you have problems with your mom?
Sara: Yeah, I guess so. A lot of people tell me I have an attitude.

Exercise: In the situation with the 18-year-old woman who had left college, how could externalizing be used?

Exercise 1: Come up with an externalization for a client problem. What questions would you ask around this externalized entity?

Exercise 2: Do you work with clients who are mandated to attend services because of the court system or are involuntary in some other way (e.g., youth with behavioral problems whose teachers or parents want them to change)? Which techniques of those discussed could you use with these clients? Using the techniques, indicate specifically what you would say.

Exercise 3: Do you work with clients who want another person to change? Which techniques of those discussed could you use with these clients? Using the techniques, indicate specifically what you would say.

CONCLUSION

Engagement is a critically important phase of the helping process. Not only does the social worker establish a basis for collaborative work, he or she sets up the purpose of the work and orients the client toward what needs to be accomplished, eliciting and building on the client's strengths. The solution-focused techniques in this chapter are useful for achieving these tasks while respectfully allowing clients to have responsibility for their own change process. The techniques discussed in this chapter provide options for you to use throughout the engagement process as well as other phases of helping. In the next section, we will turn to assessment—of clients' problems and of potential solutions.

PART 3

ASSESSMENT

CHAPTER 3

EXPLORING THE PROBLEM WITH OPEN-ENDED QUESTIONS

T he first chapter in this section on assessment will start with a discussion about questions and their importance in the helping process. Knowing how to effectively ask questions will help you explore people's problems and feelings in an in-depth way, as well as gather information about their strengths. Effective questions will also provide needed structure to client interactions and will focus the work. Finally, such questions will aid you in avoiding some of the common pitfalls that may occur in dialogue with clients. One of these pitfalls—advice giving—is discussed next.

AVOIDING ADVICE GIVING

You may have been drawn to the field of social work because people in your life have recognized your ability to listen or to give good advice. There is a key difference, however, between a helping relationship and social discourse. In the latter, we are fairly comfortable saying, "I'd do this if I were you" or "you should do this." Although social workers often need to provide education and information to clients about their problem or how to receive help for it (see Chapter 9), this step should come after allowing them to explore their experiences. Questions will help you to do this.

The following examples will illustrate what I mean by advice giving. In the first scenario, Nadia is a 17-year-old girl in foster care who is currently failing all but one of her classes.

> **Intern:** How have your grades been lately?
> **Nadia:** I don't know. I still think Ds and Fs.
> **Intern:** How about your friend from math class? Could you two help each other?

> **Nadia:** She's not very smart.
> **Intern:** How about a tutor?
> **Nadia:** Maybe, but I don't think so.

The last two intern responses are representative of advice giving. The intern first suggests that Nadia try to work with her friend from class and next that she use a tutor. Although these may be good ideas, her job is not to make suggestions to the client (who ends up rejecting these ideas anyway). We will return to this scenario again later in the book to further explore how to work with this type of situation.

A more obvious example of advice giving is presented in the following group intervention, which took place at a partial hospitalization program.

> **Julie:** Some of you know what's going on with my boyfriend. This weekend I finally came close to leaving. I not only packed the bag, but I zipped it. We had a bad weekend together. I'm just tired of him treating me any way he wants.
> **Leader:** Julie, you say this every week! You say he treats you bad and you want to leave, yet you continue to stay! Well, I guess you at least zipped the bag this week . . . looks like you're making some progress.
> **Julie:** I know, I know. Someday me and the bag will make it out the door for good!
> **Mary:** What happened this weekend?
> **Julie:** I told him that I wanted to go to a group that was for people with depression and I needed his car. He told me that I didn't need to go to the group because I was doing fine. I told him that I would be leaving here soon, and I needed another place to go for support. He refused to let me use his car. Then, I told him I had a family meeting yesterday and I wanted him to come, but he wouldn't. That's when things broke out into a big fight and I told him, "I'm tired of you treating me bad. I don't deserve you head-butting me like you did the other weekend and putting me down all the time."
> **Leader:** Again, Julie, you say you shouldn't stay with him, yet you do. What is making it so difficult for you to leave him?
> **Julie:** Well, I know I need to be on my own, but it's still hard. I just need to break up with him and concentrate on myself.
> **Brenda:** I know what you're going through, and you need to get out of that situation. When my husband and I first got married, he would put me down all the time. Then, he began hitting me and would even lock me in rooms for days at a time. I didn't get out. You need to.
> **Leader:** You see, Julie, Brenda was where you were and she made the decision to stay. You need to decide for yourself if this is what you want. You need to focus on yourself, and not on others.

In this situation, the leader directly tells the client what to do (". . . you shouldn't stay with him . . . You need to focus on yourself, and not on others") and judges the client's position (". . . yet you do. What is making it so difficult for you to leave him?").

You may be wondering why it is necessary to refrain from telling people what they should do. After all, they are coming to you for help, and you are the expert. Here are several reasons that may convince you. First, people often know what they "are supposed to do," but they are unable to follow through with this prescription, and this keeps them from moving forward. Second, advice giving also subtly conveys that the person shouldn't be so upset; after all, the problem can easily be solved with the advice you provide so quickly. In other words, advice giving minimizes their concerns.

Third, advice giving fails to take into account a person's unique experience and situation. Telling people what they "should do" implies that we know what's best for them, when they are the experts on themselves. If people choose to follow our advice, they are the ones that actually have to live with the consequences. If a social worker instructs a client to break off with his or her family in the case of sexual abuse, or to break up with an abusive boyfriend, the client may do this, believing that the social worker knows best. However, if the client is not ready to take these actions and has not been adequately prepared, he or she may end up suffering terribly from the loneliness and estrangement that may result.

Fourth, advice giving narrowly defines someone's options. There are typically many ways to handle a problem, and for a practitioner to say, "This is what you should do," limits the available options. Fifth, although people who are seeking help often ask, "What should I do?" telling them what they should do falls short of truly helping them. Clients benefit by developing their own problem-solving skills, so they can answer future questions and find solutions for themselves.

Sixth, and very importantly, offering advice can sometimes curtail the necessary expression of emotion about a situation. Jumping to advice giving is a way to stay removed from the other person's experience. In therapeutic situations, we are going for a deeper level of interaction. By allowing the client to explore and vent feelings about a situation, we are able to use empathy and enter into the client's experience. By quickly giving advice, we eliminate this aspect of the process. Exhibit 3.1 summarizes some of the disadvantages with advice giving. If telling people what to do is your natural tendency, the material in this chapter and the one on making reflecting statements that follows will help you steer away from this habitual response.

EXHIBIT 3.1: **Disadvantages of Advice Giving**

1. Minimizes people's concerns
2. Patronizes people and doesn't give them credit for having tried to solve their problems
3. Narrowly defines options
4. Curtails expression of emotions
5. Fails to take into account people's unique situations and worldviews
6. Doesn't help people develop their problem-solving capacities
7. Sometimes people already know what they need to do; the problem is that they are unable to do it.

OPEN-ENDED QUESTIONS

The use of open-ended questions is a key skill to learn. Open-ended questions involve asking a question that cannot be answered with "yes," "no," or a simple fact. They are used to gather information and to help clients explore and clarify the concerns they bring (Hepworth, Rooney, Rooney, et al., 2010). Open-ended questions allow people to explore their experiences and feelings, and they help prevent conversation from enfolding in a back-and-forth interrogative manner. Open-ended questions encourage and help clients to do their own thinking and exploring.

The use of open-ended questions is demonstrated in the following scenario. Francine is a 20-year-old young woman with a mild intellectual disability. She lives in permanent foster care with her foster mother Stacy and, until recently, Stacy's mother Miss Judy. She has experienced some difficulty adjusting since Miss Judy moved to her own apartment two weeks ago. In the following example, note how the social work intern's use of open-ended questions helps the client to openly discuss the problem behavior.

> **Intern:** What do you think we can work on today that would be helpful to you? (Open-ended question)
> **Francine:** Well, I want to move out.
> **Intern:** Can you tell me more about that? (Open-ended question)
> **Francine:** Miss Judy moved out and is living by herself.
> **Intern:** I heard about that. I guess you must miss her.
> **Francine:** Yeah, but I want to move out too.
> **Intern:** What makes you want to move out, Francine? (Open-ended question)
> **Francine:** Well, I'm old enough to do things for myself.
> **Intern:** So it sounds like you are feeling like you can take care of yourself, and you want to be more independent.
> **Francine:** Uh-huh.
> **Intern:** So, I know you left home this week without letting anyone know where you were going. Talk to me about what made you leave home by yourself. (Open-ended question)
> **Francine:** I just wanted to get a phone.
> **Intern:** I'm sure it's frustrating to you when you don't have a phone.
> **Francine:** Yeah, and Stacy wasn't getting it for me.
> **Intern:** What was the plan with Stacy about the phone? (Open-ended question)
> **Francine:** She said she was going to get it but kept changing her mind.
> **Intern:** How did Stacy feel when you left without telling her? (Open-ended question)
> **Francine:** She was probably worried.
> **Intern:** Where did you go?

Francine: I took a taxi and went to the mall and then to a fast food restaurant and then to the beauty supply store.

Intern: Wow, so you really did a lot of things by yourself. What were the good things about doing that? (Open-ended question)

Francine: I liked going to the restaurant and ordering what I wanted. And I got a new phone, but now Stacy took it away.

Intern: So it sounds like you liked making your own choices. But the phone thing didn't really work out like you wanted it to.

Francine: Right. And she says I can't have it for a week.

Intern: You know, I think if you want to talk about being more independent, you're going to have to show you can be responsible. What do you think about that? (Open-ended question)

Francine: I guess so.

Intern: What are some ways that you can show Stacy that you're ready to be more independent? (Open-ended question)

Francine: Maybe I could tell her when I'm going to the mall.

Intern: I think that's a good start. What are some other things you can start doing for yourself to show her you're being more responsible? (Open-ended question)

Francine: Hmm. I don't know. Like what?

Intern: Well, what are some of the things she does for you? (Open-ended question)

Francine: I could cook more and I could do my laundry some of the time.

Intern: Those are great ideas, Francine. How can Stacy help you get started with that? (Open-ended question)

Students often believe that because people have cognitive limitations (either because of disabilities or because they are children and have yet to develop cognitively), they cannot ask open-ended questions of them. However, the example with Francine illustrates that open-ended questioning can respectfully allow people with a range of cognitive capacity to explore their circumstances and options, without the practitioner having to make assumptions or provide the answers through the use of closed-ended questions.

Closed-ended questions are those that can be answered with either a yes/no response (e.g., "Do you like school?") or with a short piece of information (e.g., "How many brothers and sisters do you have?"). When a series of closed-ended questions is asked, the conversation unfortunately devolves into a rapid-fire pattern of questions and responses, and people do not open up about their situations. You will see in the following exercises that closed-ended questions may inadvertently act to shut down conversation rather than to allow free expression. Because people often give short responses to closed-ended questions, you will find yourself working harder when using them. Another problem with closed-ended questions is that implicit advice giving is often part of them (e.g., "Do you think you could ask your teacher?").

Students sometimes opt for closed-ended questions when collecting specific information, such as when they need to assess a client's eligibility for services or determine the types of services they need. Even in these cases, use of an open-ended question instead may put clients more at ease and encourage them to open up about their experiences.

In the example that follows, a social work intern interviewed an 18-year-old woman after she left college because of feelings of depression. The intern's purpose here is to determine the level of services the client may need. Note the use of closed-ended questions. What effect do they have on the interaction?

Intern: So what's going on?

Laura: Well, I just left college because I was feeling really depressed and was having suicidal thoughts.

Intern: How long was this going on?

Laura: It started when I got to school and had to go to the hospital down there a few weeks ago.

Intern: What hospital were you going to and how long did you stay?

Laura: I was going to Richland. I was there for three days.

Intern: Oh okay. Are you currently having these suicidal thoughts?

Laura: No.

Intern: How severe were these thoughts? Did you have a plan or ever attempt?

Laura: No, I never attempted or had a plan. I was just feeling like I didn't care.

Intern: So you were feeling hopeless?

Laura: Yeah.

Intern: Can you tell me about some of your symptoms?

Laura: I've just been really down and depressed. I haven't been able to do much.

Intern: Have you been able to sleep?

Laura: Yeah.

Intern: What about your appetite? How has that been?

Laura: I haven't been able to eat much.

Intern: Have you lost or gained any weight?

Laura: Yeah I've lost about 15 pounds since I was in the hospital.

Intern: Oh, wow. That's a lot. Do you have any substance-abuse issues?

Laura: No.

Intern: Do you have any family history of mental illnesses?

Laura: No.

Intern: Ok. What medications are you on?

Laura: [   ].

Intern: How many milligrams?

Laura: 60.

Intern: How long have you been taking it?

Laura: About three weeks.

Intern: Has it been working?

Laura: Not really.

> **Intern:** Yeah. It may need to be adjusted or need a little more time. Can you tell me what you like to do for fun?
>
> **Laura:** I like to play sports and make friendship bracelets.
>
> **Intern:** Nice. Have you made anything lately?
>
> **Laura:** Not really.
>
> **Intern:** Oh, well maybe that's something you can do when you are feeling down.

When you read this example, you may find yourself feeling that the social work intern does not convey a sense of caring to the young woman who is feeling depressed. She seems more interested in gathering specific information rather than gaining a sense of the young woman's recent experience and getting to know her better. People who are depressed may have low affect and energy, which sometimes translates to poverty of speech, but the repeated closed-ended questions only reinforce this tendency.

In the following dialogue, each of the closed-ended questions has been changed to open-ended questions. How may this have made a difference in the exchange?

> **Intern:** So what's going on?
>
> **Laura:** Well, I just left college because I was feeling really depressed and was having suicidal thoughts.
>
> **Intern:** How long was this going on?
>
> **Laura:** It started when I got to school and had to go to the hospital down there a few weeks ago.
>
> **Substitute** open-ended question: Tell me more about your thoughts and feelings during that time.
>
> **Intern:** What hospital were you going to and how long did you stay?
>
> **Laura:** I was going to [_____]. I was there for three days.
>
> **Substitute** open-ended question: Tell me about your hospital stay. What was helpful and what wasn't so helpful for you?
>
> **Intern:** Oh, okay. Are you currently having these suicidal thoughts?
>
> **Laura:** No.
>
> **Substitute** open-ended question: How are the suicidal thoughts now?
>
> **Intern:** How severe were these thoughts? Did you have a plan or ever attempt?
>
> **Note:** This seems important information to gather to assess the current level of suicidality.
>
> **Laura:** No, I never attempted or had a plan. I was just feeling like I didn't care.
>
> **Intern:** So you were feeling hopeless?
>
> **Laura:** Yeah.
>
> **Intern:** Can you tell me about some of your symptoms?
>
> **Note:** This is an open-ended question.
>
> **Laura:** I've just been really down and depressed. I haven't been able to do much.

Intern: Have you been able to sleep?
Substitute open-ended question: How is your sleep?
Laura: Yeah.
Intern: What about your appetite? How has that been?
Laura: I haven't been able to eat much.
Substitute open-ended question: Tell me about your eating patterns and weight.
Intern: Have you lost or gained any weight?
Laura: Yeah I've lost about 15 pounds since I was in the hospital.
Intern: Oh, wow. That's a lot. Do you have any substance-abuse issues?
Laura: No.
Intern: Do you have any family history of mental illnesses?
Laura: No.
Intern: Okay. What medications are you on?
Laura: [_____].
Intern: How many milligrams?
Laura: 60.
Intern: How long have you been on the medicine?
Laura: About three weeks.
Intern: Has it been working?
Laura: Not really.
Intern: Yeah. It may need to be adjusted or need a little more time. Can you tell me what you like to do for fun?
Laura: I like to play sports and make friendship bracelets.
Intern: Nice. Have you made anything lately?

Substitute open-ended question: What do you like about these hobbies?

Some closed-ended questions may be necessary so that the intern and the agency can assure the client's safety and determine the optimal level of care she needs. However, offering a greater preponderance of open-ended questions as in the example would help the client feel that the intern is interested in finding out more about her and that she will receive services from professionals who care about her well-being. The intern would also learn more about the client, including some of the strengths she brings to bear in the situation.

Exhibit 3.2 summarizes the many advantages of open-ended questions.

EXHIBIT 3.2: Advantages of Open-Ended Questions

1. Convey interest in the client
2. Allow exploration and clarification of concerns
3. Encourage exploration of feelings
4. Encourage free expression
5. Allow clients to come up with their own answers
6. Allow the client to speak more than the helper

GUIDELINES FOR ASKING OPEN-ENDED QUESTIONS

Guidelines for asking questions are summarized in Exhibit 3.3 and are elaborated upon here. First, avoid the use of "why" questions. Such questions may cause people to feel judged, accused, and may cause them to be defensive about their behaviors or circumstances (Hepworth et al., 2010). "Why?" also asks for reasons, motives, or causes that are either obvious or unknown to the client. Further, "why" questions stimulate overanalyzation of the situation and fail to encourage the exploration of feelings, thoughts, and potential resources available to the client. Instead of a "why" question, try to use "what" or "how" questions (e.g., "What do you get from raising your voice?" instead of "Why did you raise your voice?").

EXHIBIT 3.3: Guidelines for Asking Questions

Don't:	Do:
Use "why" questions	Use "how" or "what"
Ask too many questions at once	Ask one question at a time
Allow questions to predominate your repertoire	Keep the question–statement ratio at about 1:3
Allow people to speak in generalities	Ask questions to clarify specifics
Ask, "How does that *make* you feel?"	Ask, "How do you feel?"

An additional guideline for questions is to avoid asking too many of them in a row (called double-barreled questions or multiple questions). Instead, ask one question and wait for the answer. This seems obvious, but when you're nervous about a person not responding, it's easy to spout out questions. For example, an intern at a community retirement home found herself saying to Mrs. Hastings, a 93-year-old widow, "How have you been dealing with your depression? Have you been to see the psychiatrist?" When a social worker asks too many questions at once, the client may experience it as a barrage, and it might feel like an interrogation. It could also confuse the client—to which question should she respond?

Another guideline is to refrain from asking too many questions in a conversation, even open-ended ones. Beginning practitioners tend to overuse questions, since they are afraid of a possible silence. They are also more comfortable with social rather than therapeutic conversation, and the former tends to rely on questioning. Miller and Rollnick (2002) offer a rule of using one question for every three statements. Although following this guideline exactly may not be necessary, it does give you the sense that questions shouldn't predominate. Instead, you will want to rely on reflecting statements, the use of which will be discussed in the next chapter.

Another advantage of open-ended questions is that they can be used to help people be more specific about behaviors, situations, and impersonal interactions. They can be used to ask people to clarify when they speak in generalities, such as, "All bosses are out to get you." At that point, to get at specifics, you can ask questions such as "Can you give an example?" or "How did you come to that conclusion?" or "Can you tell me about the last time this happened?"

By asking for concrete details, you can explore client situations in more depth and you can work with them on changing these patterns.

Questions also allow us to ask the client about his or her feelings. However, avoid the use of the question, "How does that *make you* feel?" This question implies that the client is a victim of his or her circumstances and is powerless to choose his or her response. The phrase, from exposure in the popular media, also sounds trite. Instead, ask, "How do you feel?" which is a similar version of the question but gives the client more ownership.

Now that you've been exposed to the material and examples of open-ended questioning, you will have plenty of opportunities to practice in the following exercises.

EXERCISES

Exercise 1: Take the following and convert to open-ended questions:

1. Do you have any comments about the meals that our volunteers bring you?
2. So why couldn't you call?
3. You told me that you had some questions for the foster dad. So, did you have a chance to ask them and get answers from the dad?

Questions 1–5 involve an eight-year-old boy:

1. Did your teachers or counselors start to do anything different to help you?
2. Have there been any incidents lately?
3. Did something make you mad?
4. Have you talked to them about how you are feeling?
5. Can you try to talk to the staff at school when you are frustrated?

Questions 6–11 involve a 17-year-old girl:

6. Is there any reason why you chose to go to school in DC?
7. So you got your schedule on Friday. Did you go to class then?
8. What about today, were you in class?
9. Why didn't you want to go?
10. You were supposed to meet with the home-based therapist last week. Why weren't you home in time?
11. Do you think the attitude problem is the reason why you have problems with your mom?

> **Exercise 2**: Nadia is a 17-year-old girl in foster care who is currently failing all but one of her classes. In the following dialogue, rephrase the closed-ended questions to make them open-ended. At the end, discuss how this changes the nature of the conversation.
>
> **Intern:** How are things at school?
> **Nadia:** Fine.
> **Intern:** Do you have a lot of work to do today?
> **Nadia:** No.
> **Intern:** Can you show me what you're working on in your classes?
> **Nadia:** I didn't bring any of it home.
> **Intern:** Okay, next time I'd like to see what you're working on.
> **Nadia:** Okay, I'll try.
> **Intern:** How have your grades been lately?
> **Nadia:** I don't know. I still think Ds and Fs.
> **Intern:** What can we do to improve your grades?
> **Nadia:** I don't know.
> **Intern:** How about your friend from math class? Could you two help each other?
> **Nadia:** She's not very smart.
> **Intern:** How about a tutor?
> **Nadia:** Maybe, but I don't think so.

CONCLUSION

The use of questions is an essential tool in any social worker's interaction with clients. The information and examples in this chapter have illustrated how asking questions, particularly open-ended ones, is an excellent way to help clients experience their thoughts and feelings and expand on them in a way that closed-ended questions and statements do not. Understanding how to combine reflective listening (discussed in the next chapter) with thoughtful questions will increase your comfort level as you begin to interact with clients, and will go far in helping you uncover information and feelings that will move the helping process forward.

CHAPTER 4

EXPLORING THE PROBLEM WITH REFLECTING STATEMENTS

The preceding chapter focused on the use of questions, given their necessity for directing the conversation toward goals, strengths, and people's feelings. In this chapter the use of helping techniques that convey understanding of clients' experiences will be shown to be arguably even more important. This chapter explores these techniques—reflecting statements, showing empathy, summarizing—and variations of these that may be used to handle resistance.

REFLECTING STATEMENTS

Reflecting statements may be divided into two broad categories: reflection of content and reflection of feeling. Reflection of content involves paraphrasing—taking the factual part of a client's message—and conveying it back to the client. For example, an intern asked Mrs. Lesaca, a 67-year-old Filipino woman, how she coped with the stress of caregiving for both her aging parents. She answered, "I need God's strength. I go to church every time I can and I pray. I have a big load, but I can bear it with God." The intern used the words spoken by Mrs. Lesaca and paraphrased them into the following statement: "Your faith is something that is very important to you."

Reflection of feelings is synonymous with the expression of empathy. Empathy involves observing the emotion a person feels in the moment and conveying that experience by reflecting back the person's feelings. The use of empathy is a powerful technique for several reasons. First, it helps clients explore their emotions and experience them in more depth. Second, reflecting statements assist clients in becoming more aware of their feelings and how to identify and express them. Perhaps most importantly, reflections convey that you are listening and that you understand what the client is saying, which contributes to the working alliance.

GUIDELINES FOR REFLECTING FEELINGS

The format for reflection is "You feel [_____]." There are other lead-ins you can use that involve other sense modalities, such as:

- "It sounds like you're feeling [_____]."
- "I hear that you feel [_____]."
- "I sense you're feeling [_____]."

When I talk about feelings with clients, I refer to four main feelings: mad, sad, scared, and glad.

This keeps things simple for both children and adults who may not have a vocabulary for their emotions. Even adults with a more sophisticated vocabulary can benefit from keeping it basic with the four main feelings. This avoids the intellectualizing that may accompany higher educational levels.

Some dos and don'ts for reflecting statements are offered in Exhibit 4.1, and many examples follow in this section.

DIFFERENTIATING BETWEEN SYMPATHY AND EMPATHY

A challenge for students is to differentiate between empathy and sympathy. Sympathy involves expressing sorrow at a person's unfortunate circumstance; empathy conveys that you understand a person's emotions in the moment as they experience them. The following example demonstrates the difference between the two. Ryan is a 14-year-old, African American male who has recently returned to live with his mother and sister after staying in a residential facility for two and a half years. The intern is seeing him in home-based services. In this instance, Ryan has just completed a worksheet on feelings and thoughts.

EXHIBIT 4.1: Guidelines for Reflecting Feelings

Don't:	Do:
• Rely on the word "upset"	• Find a stronger word that more accurately conveys the emotion the client feels
• Say "I understand"	• Use a feeling word instead to convey that you understand—because you are not in the person's shoes and having the exact experience
• Say "I'm sorry"	• Reflect the feeling instead
• Use the exact words the client uses	• Paraphrase the client's words or pick up on unspoken feelings

---

> **Intern:** (reading the worksheet) So, sometimes you think that no one cares about you and that no one loves you. Next to those statements you wrote that both these make you feel very sad and hopeless. Tell me about those times when you think that no one loves you or cares about you.
>
> **Ryan:** When I'm at school, the other boys make fun of me and say that I'm a cheerleader, and that I don't act like other boys. They call me gay and faggot. It makes me feel like I don't have any friends and no one likes me. I'll never have friends, and I don't want to live anymore. I want to die. That's why I tried to kill myself before. I feel like I'm invisible.
>
> **Intern:** I'm sorry that people have been so cruel to you. No one deserves to be treated like that.
>
> **Ryan:** *silence*... I don't want to talk about this anymore.

In this instance, the intern is being sympathetic when he says, "I'm sorry that people have been so cruel to you." "I'm sorry," although well-meaning, tends to put more distance between you and the person's experience. If the intern were to use empathy, it would sound similar to the following: "It hurts so much when they call you names and bully you. You feel like you're all alone, and the pain feels like too much to handle." It's hard to say whether the empathic response would have lead to the boy being more forthcoming, but the intern's response might have caused the client to shut down ("I don't want to talk about this anymore").

REFLECTING UNSPOKEN FEELINGS

Clients will not always talk directly about their feelings. Our job is to pick up on their feelings through the words they use and their body language. For example, an intern placed at a retirement community worked with 87-year-old Mrs. Lustre, who said, "My family doesn't visit me and call me that much. I have one niece that calls me pretty regularly, but she's not the one that I am really close to. Oh, well, that's just how it is." The intern responded, "You feel neglected because your family doesn't call you often." Although the client did not state her feelings directly (in fact, she minimized them by saying, "that's just how it is"), the intern picked up on the underlying feeling and stated it back to her.

In another example, an intern worked with Cathy, a 37-year-old Caucasian female who has been diagnosed with major depressive disorder. Although she takes medication, she continues to struggle with depression. She has not been in therapy for a year but recently expressed interest in returning to her last therapist.

> **Intern:** I spoke to your old therapist yesterday, and, unfortunately, she does not have any openings to take new clients on.
>
> **Cathy:** Oh.
>
> **Intern:** I can hear in your voice how disappointed you are about that.
>
> **Cathy:** I am. I really trusted her.

The intern conveys, in this exchange, that she is attuned to the client's emotional state. Because she first validated the client's feelings, the intern may be able to explore the client's options for getting on a waitlist for that particular therapist, or for seeing someone new or on a temporary basis. However, without having her feelings validated, the client would likely be unwilling to move on to problem solving.

The final example in this section involves a relapse prevention group at an outpatient substance abuse treatment facility.

PJ: I'm PJ. I'm here because of my parole. I recently got out of prison for a sex offense.

Justin: Do you always have to mention that you molested a nine-year-old boy? We don't want to hear about how perverted you are. This group is about dealing with our addiction, not your past sex life.

PJ: My sex offender group in prison taught us to share our experiences because keeping it a secret will only cause us more problems. And I did not say that I molested anyone.

Justin: We know you did.

Leader: Justin, can you tell PJ how it makes you feel when he talks about his offense?

Justin: It makes me feel like punching you. It turns my stomach.

Leader: So you feel mad and uncomfortable.

Note that Justin speaks in harsh language to the fellow group member about his reaction, but the leader translates, or reframes, his words into feeling words ("mad" and "uncomfortable"). In this way, she teaches him (and the other group members) how to recognize and verbalize these feelings. Next, a longer scenario will be presented, so you can see how reflecting can be utilized with great effect throughout an exchange.

In a hospice setting, an intern worked with Dana, a client whose father died five months prior.

Dana: I just keep thinking about the last few weeks before he died, especially the last night that he was in the hospital.

Intern: You are really sad about how quickly your father declined before he died.

Dana: Yes. We think that he must have had a stroke. He lost his hearing after the night he lost so much blood in the hospital. He had already lost his sense of smell and taste, but when he lost his hearing, well, he just gave up after that.

Intern: You're so frustrated that the hospital didn't take care of his nosebleed and sad that he gave up fighting for his life.

Dana: I just wonder what it was like for him. I wonder if he was scared.

Intern: You're so heartbroken about how things happened in the last few weeks of his life.

> **Dana:** It was really horrible. The hospital just let him sit there bleeding all night. The doctors barely saw him at all. He lost several pints of blood that night. I filed a complaint about the service because I really didn't think that they did a whole lot to help him. I will never go to that hospital again. I will go out of my way to avoid that place.
> **Intern:** You're angry about how your father was treated at the hospital.
> **Dana:** Yeah. Then the hospital sent me a letter saying that I wasn't legally able to receive the information about the outcome of the complaint.
> **Intern:** You were frustrated that the hospital didn't give you information about the complaint.
> **Dana:** Yeah. I don't know if they did anything or if they just sided with the doctors and just threw my letter away.
> **Intern:** You felt ignored and discounted.

In this dialogue, the reflective statements demonstrate that the intern understands Dana's emotional pain and her complaints. In doing so, the intern continues to build rapport with the client and nurture the therapeutic relationship, offering her a safe environment in which to grieve.

REFLECTING CLIENT'S ANGER TOWARD *YOU*

A particularly difficult situation is making reflecting statements when the client's anger is directed at you. Our natural human response in these situations is to become defensive and argue our position. However, that is not a therapeutic response. Instead, we have to remain calm, at least outwardly, and give the client the opportunity to explore his or her feelings in a safe environment. At the same time, you do not have to allow abuse. If clients are calling you names or swearing at you, of course you must tell them to stop this behavior, and if they do not, you can leave the situation.

The following example involves Jada, a 17-year-old African American female in foster care. Her two-year-old daughter, Brianna, currently lives with Jada's mother, but Jada is trying to obtain custody of her daughter. First, the scenario will run as it actually occurred. Then you will see how it might have proceeded with the addition of reflecting statements in the intern's responses.

> **Jada:** My mom's social worker told her that you all want me to have Brianna during the week.
> **Intern:** Well, as you know we had a meeting last week, and we brought up the idea of having you keep Brianna more so you could see what it's like to have her full-time. Are you not okay with that idea?

> **Jada:** Well, how are you going to expect me to go to school and then to work and then get Brianna? Why are you going to tell my mother that I want to do something like that?
>
> **Intern:** Jada, I have never talked with your mother. I also have never talked with her social worker. One of the reasons I was calling you was to talk about a time to meet with you to talk about our meeting last week, and to talk to you about me possibly meeting your mother at some point.
>
> **Jada:** I don't care about that. I'm just saying that I don't know how y'all expect me to take care of Brianna during the week with my job and school.
>
> **Intern:** We aren't going to force you to do something you don't want to do. If you don't want to have Brianna more often, then you don't have to. We thought that since you wanted to get custody of Brianna that this would be something you would be interested in. It would allow you to see what it would be like to have her around the clock.
>
> **Jada:** No, I never said I wanted that.
>
> **Intern:** And again, you don't have to if you don't want to. However, I will say that when you go to court in January and the judge asks us if you were given the chance to have Brianna more than the weekends, we will have to tell him or her that you were given the chance to have her more than just weekends but that you did not want to. I just need for you to understand that he or she will probably ask us that question.
>
> **Jada:** I don't care! Can you call back some other time during the week or something? I don't want to talk about this anymore.

In this conversation, both the social work intern and Jada respond to each other defensively: Jada repeats her position of not wanting to care for Brianna more often, and the social worker keeps talking about the need for Jada to take on more responsibility. The social worker does not acknowledge Jada's apprehension about the responsibilities she already faces and instead continues with her own agenda.

Here is the hypothetical scenario with the addition of reflecting statements. Some of the client's dialogue has also been changed to illustrate how her addiction might have changed the nature of the interaction.

> **Jada:** My mom's social worker told her that you all want me to have Brianna during the week.
>
> **Intern:** Well, as you know we had a meeting last week, and we brought up the idea of having you keep Brianna more so you could see what it's like to have her full-time. Are you not okay with that idea?
>
> **Jada:** Well, how are you going to expect me to go to school and then work and then get Brianna? Why you going to tell my mother that I want to do something like that?

Intern reflecting statement: It sounds like you are overwhelmed by the idea of school, work, and taking care of Brianna, and you are angry because you think the social workers are making plans behind your back.

Jada: That's right. I don't know how I'm going to do all that. I mean, I want to have Brianna more, but nobody knows what it's like to try to go to school and work and have a baby.

Intern reflecting statement: You are worried that you won't be able to handle all the responsibility.

Jada: Right. But that doesn't mean I don't love my daughter or want to be with her more, like the social workers are making it sound.

Intern reflecting statement: You are afraid your concerns are not being heard.

Jada: It makes me so mad. Everybody's having all these meetings trying to figure out what I need to do, and nobody's asking me. Everyone thinks I need to have Brianna all the time and still do everything I have to do.

Intern reflecting statement: You are angry because you feel like you are being pressured into taking Brianna more often.

Through substituting reflective statements in the dialogue, Jada has the opportunity to openly discuss her worries about caring for Brianna more often. The social worker is no longer seen as defensive and siding with the other social workers against Jada. She is able to build trust and align herself with her client through hearing Jada's feelings about the added responsibility of caring for Brianna.

EXERCISES

Exercise 1: Recall the example of Laura, the young woman who left college because of depression. The original exchange relied almost entirely on questions. Insert reflecting statements into the dialogue. How does their addition change the interaction between the intern and Laura?

Intern: So what's going on?

Laura: Well, I had to leave college because I was feeling really depressed and was having suicidal thoughts.

Intern: How long has this been going on?

Laura: It started right after I got to school, and then I had to go to the hospital down there a few weeks ago.

Intern: What hospital did you go to and how long did you stay?

Laura: I went to [_____], and I was there for three days.

Intern: Okay. So are you currently having these suicidal thoughts?

Laura: No.

Intern: How severe were these thoughts? Did you have a plan or ever attempt suicide?

Laura: No, I never attempted or had a plan. I was just feeling like I didn't care.

Intern: So you felt hopeless?

Laura: Yeah.

Intern: Can you tell me about some of your symptoms?

Laura: I've just been really down and depressed. I haven't been able to do much.

Intern: Have you been able to sleep?

Laura: Yeah.

Intern: What about your appetite? How has that been?

Laura: I haven't been able to eat much.

Intern: Have you lost or gained any weight?

Laura: Yeah, I've lost about 15 pounds since I was in the hospital.

Intern: Oh, wow. That's a lot. Do you have any substance-abuse issues?

Laura: No.

Intern: Do you have any family history of mental illness?

Laura: No.

Intern: Ok. What medications are you taking?

Laura: I'm on [_____].

Intern: How many milligrams?

Laura: 60.

Intern: How long have you been taking it?

Laura: About three weeks.

Intern: Has it been working?

Laura: Not really.

Intern: Yeah. They may need to adjust it or it may need a little more time.

Intern: Can you tell me what you like to do for fun?

Laura: I like to play sports and make friendship bracelets.

Intern: Nice. Have you made anything lately?

Laura: Not really.

Intern: Oh, well maybe that's something you can do when you are feeling down.

Exercise 2: Sara is a 17-year-old adolescent and the mother of two-year-old Maggie. She has a history of truancy and is enrolled in ninth grade at an alternative school. Sara currently lives with her mother, Rachelle. In the following scenario, construct statements that show empathy for this mother's concerns.

Intern: How have things been since I was here last week?

Rachelle: Bad. Sara left Maggie here on Friday and didn't tell anyone where she was going. She didn't come back till late and then she left again at 10 a.m. on Saturday and didn't come home until 5 p.m. last night. She said she was going to the store. It doesn't take you that long to go to the store.

Intern: She didn't tell anyone where she was going?

Rachelle: No. We all tried calling her, but she didn't pick up her phone, didn't answer texts. She doesn't follow the rules. She doesn't listen. Sara does what Sara wants to do.

Intern: It seems like she doesn't listen to you at all. What would you want your relationship with her to be?

Rachelle: Perfect.

Intern: Explain what you mean by perfect.

Rachelle: When she doesn't lie. Answer her phone when we call her. She says I don't know how to talk to her. She does what she wants. She wants to be a mother, but how can she? I told her she needs to read the Bible or something.

Intern: So you want a relationship where she communicates with you more. Do you do things as a family?

Rachelle: Oh yeah, but she doesn't ever participate. We go to the movies, bowling, and laser tag.

Intern: It sounds like you do a lot of activities together. Why doesn't Sara ever participate?

Rachelle: Because she's never around and she has such a bad attitude that nobody wants her to come' cause she'll ruin the mood.

Intern: So everyone else does things together, but Sara is left out?

Rachelle: Yeah' cause she doesn't want to participate.

Intern: Is there ever a time that she will participate? Tell me about those times.

Rachelle: We just talk. Joke around. We won't yell at each other, just be normal.

Intern: Why do you think that doesn't happen often?

Rachelle: Because she has an attitude problem. She's nice when she wants to be.

Intern: She acknowledges the fact that she has an attitude.

Rachelle: She doesn't care. A while ago she got a ride from her sister and stole money out of the glove compartment. My older daughter knew how much money was in there. She had no reason to lie.

Intern: Do you know why she would be stealing?

Rachelle: I try to buy her things to make her happy, but it's never good enough. She's just disrespectful.

Exercise 3: In the following scenario, Caitlin, a 12-year-old girl, has just recounted sexual abuse by her stepfather to the CPS/police system. Insert a reflecting statement in place of each of the social work intern's responses.

Intern: How are you doing?

Caitlin: Not good.

Intern: Do you feel better now that you've told your mom?

Caitlin: No. I ruined everything. I broke up the family. Why couldn't she [the investigative caseworker] just tell my mom? It's so disgusting and embarrassing. I hate it.

Intern: You didn't do anything wrong. You were brave to talk about it. You stopped this from continuing. He did this; you didn't do anything. We needed you to tell your mom because she trusts you. We didn't want her to think we were putting words in your mouth. It means more for your mom to hear it from you.

Caitlin: I just want to go under the covers and melt away and never come back. It's all my fault. I ruined the family. I should've stopped him. I should've killed him. I just want to go away.

Intern: It's not your fault. You didn't want this to happen to you. He's an adult; he should know better. He should have never touched you in the first place.

Caitlin: I just want to go home.

Intern: Are you sure you want to go home or do you want to go to your dad's?

Caitlin: I want to go to my room and not come out for days and just die of starvation.

EXERCISES FOR YOUR PRACTICE

Exercise 1: Think of a client with whom you are currently working (or one you have seen in the past if you do not yet have client contact). Come up with two reflecting statements.

1.
2.

Exercise 2: Think of a client with whom you are currently working (or one you have seen in the past if you do not yet have client contact) that may have been angry at you (you can create a hypothetical case if you haven't yet had this experience). Come up with two reflecting statements you could make if the client were angry at you:

1.
2.

HANDLING "RESISTANCE" WITH REFLECTIVE LISTENING

You may hear a lot from supervisors and fellow agency workers about "resistance"—when clients deny their problem or interrupt, ignore or argue with the practitioner. Such behaviors can be difficult to manage. However, resistance is defined in both motivational interviewing and solution-focused therapy as "not being on the same page as the client." Resistance, therefore, is seen not as the client's problem, but as a signal that the practitioner needs to change strategies. Miller and Rollnick (2002) have created helper responses to sidestep resistance. These responses are variations of reflective listening, but with a directive component that moves the interaction away from a power struggle and instead toward change. These responses will be described below and illustrated with the following scenario:

Mrs. Hall is a 33-year-old African American single parent with three children, ages 15, 11, and 7. She had been receiving TANF (Temporary Assistance for Needy Families) assistance for the past three years since her husband deserted her. The intern writes, "During the past year, my agency made several efforts to get her a job, without success. The records showed that Mrs. Hall did not want to get a job, as she felt she was too busy taking care of her children, but the truth is that she is aware that getting a job will reduce her TANF check. I had the following conversation with her in other to motivate her to get a job."

> **Intern:** What would you like to see yourself doing 10 years from now?
> **Mrs. Hall:** I haven't given it much thought.
> **Intern:** What about your current situation; how satisfied are you with it?
> **Mrs. Hall:** I am not satisfied about my life now; it is very difficult to live on this inadequate TANF budget, to raise three children all by myself, and all the stress that comes from my husband deserting us.

> **Intern:** I understand your concerns. It's true that past events have led to your current situation, but how you want your present and future to be will depend largely on you.
>
> **Mrs. Hall:** How do you mean?
>
> **Intern:** Take your financial situation, for example; you have a choice between staying at home and seeking a job. If you don't begin to learn an employable skill now and gradually work your way up in the job, what's going to happen in 10 years when you will no longer be eligible for the TANF payments?
>
> **Mrs. Hall:** It would be nice to get a job, but there are also many reasons why it would not be possible for me to get a job.
>
> **Intern:** Tell me more about that.
>
> **Mrs. Hall:** Eventually, if I work, it would not add to my total income, because my TANF check will be reduced. I have also tried finding a job several times in the past and wasn't successful. I wouldn't be able to work and also take care of my home and family.
>
> **Intern:** Having failed in the past doesn't mean you can't be successful this time. I hope you've heard the saying "if at first you don't succeed, try, try again." I encourage you to try again.

In this exchange, the social work intern's attempts to convince Mrs. Hall that she needs to get a job have little impact, and they come across as lecturing. Mrs. Hall is prepared with a response for each of the intern's suggestions that she should work, and the intern and client both try to assert their opinions. The following section on the different types of reflection will illustrate the various options available to us that help move our clients away from resistance and toward change.

SIMPLE REFLECTION

In order to prevent the power struggle that results in the above exchange, you could use a *simple reflection*, typically a paraphrase of what the client has been saying. Simple reflection involves acknowledgment of a client's feeling, thought, or opinion so that the client continues to explore his or her problem rather than becoming defensive. An example of a *simple reflection* with Mrs. Hall is: "It is very difficult to live on the inadequate TANF budget."

When using reflection, make sure to reflect the part of clients' statements that allow them to take responsibility for their actions rather than the part of their statement that blames others (Bertolino & O'Hanlon, 2002). For instance, a man who was referred to a batterer intervention program talked about how his wife was "always nagging" and he "finally snapped and pushed her." Rather than saying, "Your wife was really irritating you and you had it," you would emphasize his actions: "You lost control of your anger and you pushed your wife." Since our work often involves helping people be accountable for their actions, the selection of what part of a client's message we reflect back is key.

AMPLIFIED REFLECTION

A variation of the reflective response is to make an *amplified reflection*, in which the client's resistance is slightly overstated. This takes advantage of a person's natural tendency to speak against either side of a decision about which he or she is ambivalent. It is likely to produce a verbal backpedaling toward a less entrenched opinion where negotiation is possible. The value of an amplified reflection is that the client, rather than the practitioner, makes the argument toward the desired change. An example of *amplified reflection* with Mrs. Hall is as follows: "Not finding a job the times you've tried probably means you will never find a job that meets your income needs." This statement might cause Mrs. Hall to take the other side of this statement, bringing out the part of her that may be more receptive to finding a job.

DOUBLE-SIDED REFLECTION

Double-sided reflection reflects both aspects of the client's ambivalence—the experience of being divided between wanting to change and wanting to keep the behavior that has become problematic. Double-sided reflection can pull the client's attention to the inconsistency between the problem behavior and his or her goals and values (Moyers & Rollnick, 2002): "So you're not happy with the TANF program, and you're not willing to look for a job and get off the program because you will lose the money and won't have the benefits if you get a job."

SHIFTING FOCUS

Shifting focus involves moving the client's attention away from his or her position in order to avoid a potential impasse. When the client begins to argue against what the practitioner might feel is the best course, the practitioner should immediately shift his or her position and redirect the focus. The general guideline for shifting focus "is to first defuse the initial concern and then direct attention to a more readily workable issue" (Miller & Rollnick, 2002, p. 102). An example with Mrs. Hall would be as follows: "Let's not talk about cutting off your benefits; let's just explore your current position on job training and the kind of work you may be interested in pursuing in the future."

AGREEMENT WITH A TWIST

Another strategy, *agreement with a twist*, involves agreement with some of the client's message, but in a way that then orients the client in the direction toward change. An example of the use of agreement with a twist with Mrs. Hall is as follows: "You're right. The TANF budget is totally inadequate. It's not enough to live on. Most jobs would pay more."

CLARIFYING FREE CHOICE

Clarifying free choice communicates the fact that it is up to the client whether he or she wants to change, rather than getting embroiled in a debate or an argument about what the client must do. For Mrs. Hall, a statement such as the following clarifies free choice: "It's really up to you whether you want to look for work." "When people perceive that their freedom of choice is being threatened, they tend to react by asserting their liberty. Probably the best antidote for this reaction is to assure the person of what is surely the truth: in the end, it is the client who determines what happens" (Miller & Rollnick, 2002, p. 106).

EXERCISES

MULTIPLE-CHOICE QUESTIONS

1. **Client:** I don't know what to do. I suppose I need to leave him for the sake of my son, but I can't afford to raise him by myself.
   Intern: You're concerned about how you'd be able to manage financially without him.
   In the above instance, what kind of response does the practitioner use?
   A. Simple reflection
   B. Amplified reflection
   C. Double-sided reflection
   D. Clarifying free choice

2. The interaction continues here from the scenario in 1.
   Client: I want to deal with my problems, but sometimes I think it would be easier not to bother.
   Intern: On one hand, you don't want to be here, and on the other hand, you want help for your problems.
   In the above instance, what kind of response does the practitioner use?
   A. Simple reflection
   B. Amplified reflection
   C. Double-sided reflection
   D. Clarifying free choice

3. The following exchange is another instance of work with a victim of intimate partner violence.
   Client: My husband is a decent man.
   Intern: Your husband would never hurt you.
   In the above instance, what kind of response does the practitioner use?
   A. Simple reflection
   B. Amplified reflection

C. Double-sided reflection
D. Clarifying free choice
4. The exchange from 3 continues here.
Client: I wouldn't say "never." But he feels bad when he does it.
Intern: Your husband hurts you.
In the above instance, what kind of response does the practitioner use?
A. Simple reflection
B. Amplified reflection
C. Double-sided reflection
D. Clarifying free choice

EXERCISE FOR YOUR PRACTICE

In the following exercise, provide examples of "resistance" that you have seen from clients (or that you have heard your colleagues and supervisors discuss). In the last column, write in one of the reflective/strategic responses discussed in the last section.

Signs	Description[1]	Client Example	Technique to Handle Resistance
Arguing	Client questions or disagrees with the practitioner's stance or credentials.		
Interrupting	Client cuts off or talks over the practitioner in an inappropriate or defensive manner.		
Denial	Client fails to recognize issues, participate, or take responsibility. Client blames, disagrees, finds excuses, minimizes. Client presents with hopelessness about changing or is not willing to change.		
Ignoring	Client fails to track the practitioner's speech, doesn't answer, or derails the line of discussion.		

[1] These are from Miller & Rollnick (2002).

SUMMARIZING

Summarizing is the final skill to be discussed in this chapter. Summarizing is similar to paraphrasing but involves a longer amount of speech. Hepworth et al. (2010) suggests that summarizing can be particularly beneficial when a client has talked at some length or his or her speech is tangential, rambling, or confused. Hearing the social worker recount their own thoughts helps clients organize what may feel overwhelming to them. It also clarifies your understanding of their statements. In this way, summarizing can add direction and coherence to your contact with a client. Summarizing is also helpful when you are switching directions or ending a contact with a client so that you can sum up what has been discussed. As always, you will want to emphasize strengths and progression toward goals.

In the following example, an intern placed at a child welfare agency drove Ruth, a 50-year-old Caucasian woman, to an appointment.

Intern: So what led you to the Department of Human Services (DHS)?

Ruth: The court did, not me. I don't want to have anything to do with these DHS people; they're all a bunch of liars.

Intern: Are you saying that it's the court's decision for you to come into the DHS system?

Ruth: Yes, but not for me. I would not come into this darned social service system, if not for my grandchildren.

Intern: What about them?

Ruth: They've put three of them in some foster home, and they are starving to death; they've all lost weight and look skinny. I am ready to go to all lengths and get them back… I'm not playing. I can't live without them; I've lived with them since they were babies, and now I live by myself and without them. I am frustrated.

Intern: You mean you want custody of your grandchildren?

Ruth: Sure, that's what I'm doing right now. I have a court date soon. I'm sure to have them back.

Intern: What lead to DHS taking over three of your grandchildren?

Ruth: DHS did not take over those kids. I applied to the court to take two of those children, ages 11 and 16, whom are out of control, but when DHS came to pick them up, they took the third one too. Now I want them back. I live alone in my house, and it gets boring without them.

Intern: Let me see if I've got what you're saying. You asked for help with the two oldest children because you found it hard to manage them, but then you feel like you lost control of the situation because DHS put the third one into foster care as well. Now you miss them terribly, and you're worried about their well-being. You'll do anything you can to get them back home.

Note in this summarizing statement how the intern concentrates on facts (asking for help) and the client's feelings (loss of control, miss them terribly, worried). She also orients the client toward achievement of goals ("you'll do anything you can to get them back home").

Another example involves an intern who was placed in a continuing care retirement community. The intern worked with Mrs. Moody, an 84-year-old Caucasian who was diagnosed with dementia. In this instance, the social worker and intern meet with Mrs. Moody's 65-year-old daughter, Beth, and her husband, Perry.

Beth: (Pulls out a piece of paper) On Saturday starting at 10:02 a.m., my mother called inquiring how she would be getting to our house that afternoon. She said that she had gone down to the garage and found that her car was no longer there. Perry told her that we had sold her car because she was no longer able to drive. She asked who decided that she could no longer drive, and we told her the doctor. She said she wasn't sure about that and would have to talk to the doctor and get back to us. At 10:34 she called back again asking what had happened to her car. We explained again that she was no longer able to drive. She didn't believe us. At 11:14 she called again asking if we were going to pick her up. She can't find her car and is very agitated. We told her that we would pick her up at 1:00 p.m. and we could discuss the car then. She got very angry, demanding to know why we had taken her car. Another call came in at 12:30 and...

Perry: I think they get the idea, Beth. They know already about the situation with her and the car.

Beth: Well, when we brought her over to the house she was upset because she wanted to eat out instead. She came in and sat down at the table for five minutes and then got up and wandered around the house saying that she was bored. I told her to come back and eat with us, but she refused. She went from room to room looking for something to do until 2:30 p.m., when she said she was tired of being in the house. We took her back to her apartment. Then she began calling us again about the car. Then—

Intern: I'm sorry to interrupt, but what I'm hearing from you is that it is very frustrating and tiring dealing with the constant calling and the behaviors brought on by the dementia.

In this scenario, the social worker summarizes after a lengthy expression of anger and frustration by Beth. She validates Beth's concerns and experiences with Mrs. Moody. It is important to note, as in this example, that you may politely interrupt a person who has been going on for some time. Although people need to be heard and understood for their experiences, your job is to also structure the interaction so that it is productive.

CONCLUSION

This chapter has focused on reflecting clients' statements and the different variations of this technique. Reflecting statements, perhaps more than any other strategy we use as social workers, are integral to the helping process and are used in all phases of the process. Until clients feel heard and understood, our work with them will be limited. Reflecting statements help social workers move the conversation forward and keep us from becoming polarized with our clients. These last two chapters encourage you to effectively learn to use reflecting statements and to pair them with open-ended questions. Doing so will help you open the door to clients' feelings, information, willingness to change, and ultimately to the solutions of their problems.

CHAPTER 5

EXPLORING THE ADVANTAGES AND DISADVANTAGES OF THE PROBLEM AND CHANGE

Social workers often have clients who have been referred to them for problem behaviors, such as anger control, child abuse, substance use, sexual risk-taking, and medication noncompliance. The decisional balance, a way of assessing such problems, is the focus of this chapter. Taken from motivational interviewing, the decisional balance allows for nonjudgmental exploration of the problem rather than confrontation and blame and avoids putting the worker in a lecturing or authoritative role (Miller & Rollnick, 2002). In this way, clients are invited to speak nondefensively about their behavior while maintaining a collaborative relationship with their helper. The decisional balance can also help build people's motivation to change.

STEPS OF THE DECISIONAL BALANCE

Essentially, decisional balance explores the advantages and disadvantages of continuing the problem behavior and examines the advantages and disadvantages of changing. Following is a description of the steps to take with decisional balance (Miller & Rollnick, 2002):

STEP 1: ASSESS THE ADVANTAGES OF THE PROBLEM BEHAVIOR

When clients first begin to work on a problem behavior, they may feel defensive about the behavior and worry that the practitioner is going to tell them what to do. Beginning the process by examining the advantages of the problem behavior is helpful because it is less threatening. Asking the client what they like about their behavior or "what they get out of it" disarms the defensiveness. People enjoy having their perspective heard and, as a consequence, feel less judged by the practitioner.

They are also given credit for the fact that the problem behavior, although seemingly irrational and perhaps even destructive, must serve some key purposes in order for the problem to remain in place. Therefore, in addition to helping clients feel more understood, "asking about the advantages" can help the social worker learn about the needs that the problem behavior meets. For example, if a person reports that she uses alcohol to combat her depression, the social worker learns that assisting the client with mood problems will be an important goal. As another example, people sometimes report that drinking eases the strain of talking to others. In this situation, the social worker may note that the client needs help with social skills and ways to reduce anxiety without resorting to alcohol.

The following excerpt shows the benefits of allowing the client to explore his or her own reasons for the problem behavior. This conversation between Kate, a 17-year-old, and a caseworker takes place after she has been admitted to an inpatient psychiatric hospital due to a suicide attempt. Here she describes what lead to the attempt.

Kate: I was drunk and not thinking. My dad and I got in an argument over something stupid and then he called the police and, of course, I got another underage drinking citation.
Caseworker: What happened after that?
Kate: I took some pills 'cause I didn't feel like dealing with all that court stuff again.
Caseworker: Were you doing any other drugs that night?
Kate: Yeah, I smoked some weed. I don't know why drinking and smoking is such a big deal. Everyone does it.
Caseworker: I don't know if everyone does it, but it is illegal to smoke marijuana and to drink under the age of 21, and often people drink and do drugs for one of three reasons. They do it to feel better, different, or nothing at all. Do you feel you do drugs for any of these reasons?
Kate: I like drinking and smoking with my friends, but it also helps me deal with my crazy mother.

In this example, the caseworker seemed to be lecturing Kate when he told her it was illegal to smoke, a fact Katie surely already knows. One must refrain from lecturing or preaching to clients, as it is a polarizing, rather than a collaborative, position to take. Instead, asking clients what they get out of using substances conveys that you are interested in learning their motives rather than judging them for their behavior. In the example, the caseworker suggests that people use substances for one of three reasons. Here he offers general observations rather than learning about his client's individual reasons. You can see that Kate refuses to be pigeonholed by his remarks and states that her reasons are outside what he has offered when she says, "I like drinking and smoking with my friends, but it also helps me deal with my crazy mother." The caseworker could have then reflected back, "So it's something you enjoy doing with your friends and perhaps helps you connect with your friends. And you also have a hard time dealing with your mother, and drinking and smoking help you cope with that. What else does drinking and smoking do for you?" In this way, the clinician could gain a better understanding of the client, further the relationship between them, and lower her defensiveness. He also could learn about what Kate might be interested in working on, such as relating to peers in a way that doesn't involve substances and/or managing and improving her family circumstances.

STEP 2: DISADVANTAGES OF THE PROBLEM BEHAVIOR

In the process of talking about what clients like about their problem behavior, they will sometimes spontaneously initiate discussion of its downsides. If not, you can say, "Now that we've talked about what you get out of [the drug use, not taking your medication, purging after meals], let's talk about the not-so-good things." When people turn to the disadvantages of their behavior, they should be encouraged to speak about these at some length, giving concrete examples. For instance, you could say, "You've said you don't like the way you act when you've been drinking a lot. Can you give me a recent example of when this happened?" By describing in detail specific incidences, people begin to hear how the problem behavior has landed them into services. Other questions you can ask to get the client to think of the disadvantages include the following (Miller & Rollnick, 2002):

- What things make you think (your problem) is a problem?
- In what ways do you think you or other people have been harmed by your (problem)?
- How has your (problem) stopped you from doing what you want to do?

In the example of Kate, after talking about what she gets out of "drinking and smoking," she might be more amenable to sharing some of the disadvantages of her behavior. For instance, she tried to commit suicide when she was under the influence of alcohol and drugs. Also, her substance use seemed to cause arguments in the family and allowed her parents think that the only problem was her drug use and not the family circumstances. As a result, they tended to over-focus on her substance use and not give any attention to their interaction patterns.

STEP 3: ADVANTAGES OF CHANGING

The first two steps described above are probably the most essential parts of the decisional balance, but you can also go on to explore the advantages of changing, the third step in the decisional balance. Here you can make such statements as: "The fact that you're here indicates that at least a part of you thinks it's time to do something. What are the reasons you see for making a change? What are the good things about changing?" (Miller & Rollnick, 2002). In discussing the advantages, you can highlight the clients' values and goals for their lives, such as their children, their other relationships, and their professional aspirations, and how change may allow for the expression of these values and goals.

STEP 4: DISADVANTAGES OF CHANGING

The final step in the decisional balance is to talk about the disadvantages of changing. The disadvantages are important to address because they can show up later as stumbling blocks if they have not been discussed explicitly with the client. Although there will be individual reasons dictated by your client, his or her circumstances, and unique experiences and preferences, here are some common reasons why people don't like change:

- The effort involved in changing, forging new habits, and making a new routine is too great.
- Although change may be desirable, it's also scary because it's an unknown. The problem feels comfortable and familiar, in contrast.
- Some people will feel as if they are losing a significant part of themselves, their identity, if they make a change.
- Some people resent being told what to do, even if another part of them (the part that wants to change) is telling them what to do. To show they are in charge, they rebel against plans and efforts to change.
- They don't know how to go about changing.
- They might lose people who are important to them (for example, a woman who abuses drugs may know she will have to leave her drug-dealing boyfriend in order to quit; people whose social life is gathered around a problem, such as drinking, may recognize that they will have to leave this circle of friends in order to stay sober).

EXAMPLES OF DECISIONAL BALANCE

Below are a few examples of the decisional balance. The first two are generic problems that social workers may encounter in practice—the use of physical punishment as a child discipline method (Exhibit 5.1) and women who are in violent relationships (Exhibit 5.2). Although a decisional balance must be individualized to the particular client, as each person will hold unique perspectives toward the advantages and disadvantages of the problem behavior and to changing it, these generic templates can be helpful. Some generalities can be made about what holds a particular problem, such as physical discipline and violence in an intimate relationship, in place. Following these examples is a unique situation that arose out of a child protective services investigation.

EXHIBIT 5.1: Sample Decisional Balance for Leaving an Abusive Relationship

Benefits of Continuing to Stay in the Relationship	Costs of Continuing to Stay in the Relationship	Benefits of Leaving the Relationship	Costs of Leaving the Relationship
Gets love, attention, affection, and companionship	Physical injury	Increased self-esteem and self-respect	Loneliness
Obtains financial support	Emotional problems	Physical safety	Fear of the unknown
Has a father figure for the children	Feels worse about self	Focus on parenting rather than the relationship	Fear of retaliation
Only happens periodically, combined with loving, contrite behavior at other times[1]	Poor role modeling for children	Gain respect of children	Lack of financial support
If abuser is the father of children, continuous contact anyway for the sake of the children[1]	Lack of stability/ security in home	Build a better social support network	Give up house/ residence
He might follow through on his promises to change	Possible intergenerational cycle of abuse		Have to find/ maintain a place to stay
No other place to stay	Isolation (hiding the effects of the abuse, shame)		

[1] Fernandez et al. (1997)

EXHIBIT 5.2: Decisional Balance with Physical Discipline
Note: For simplicity, only one side of the decisional balance may be completed as in this example.

Advantages of Physical Discipline	Disadvantages of Physical Discipline
1. Children obey.	For the parent
2. Release of anger is a relief.	1. Guilt
3. Children know who's in charge/respect parents.	2. Possible legal consequences
4. Parents want children to succeed in life and to be tough against adversity; they believe that physical discipline is a way to achieve these goals.	3. Outside involvement in family life, such as child protective services investigation
	4. May cause intergenerational transmission of aggression; e.g., continuing the cycle of aggression[1]
5. People's parents may have physically abused them, so they believe it is an appropriate way to manage children's misbehavior.	For the child
	5. Children may feel negatively toward the person enacting the punishment and toward the source of the behaviors for which they are being punished (e.g., homework, other siblings).

6. Teaches children aggression by modeling aggression
7. Children learn what they shouldn't do, but not what they should do.
8. Research findings indicate physical abuse is correlated for children with 1) aggression/behavior problems; 2) poor impulse control; 3) social skills deficits; 4) cognitive deficits in terms of language and IQ/academic problems; 5) trauma-related symptoms, such as anxiety and depression[2]

[1] Deater-Deckard, Dodge, & Sorbring (2005)
[2] Kolko & Swenson (2002)

Exhibit 5.3: The following decisional balance was completed with a 44-year-old single mother of a five-year-old girl. She was referred to CPS after police noted that she seemed somewhat intoxicated when they visited for a noise complaint from a fellow neighbor in the apartment building where they lived. The decisional balance investigates the advantages and disadvantages of her drinking behavior and the possibility of change.

The client enjoyed some of the perceived benefits she received from drinking wine and was reluctant to relinquish them. Therefore, she may be a candidate for behavioral self-control, an approach that advocates limited drinking rather than total abstinence (Mirin et al., 2006). She was also educated on the health benefits of two glasses of wine a day but that in excess may pose health risks (Di Castelnuovo et al., 2006).

EXHIBIT 5.3: Sample Client Decisional Balance

Advantages of Problem Behavior	Disadvantages of Problem Behavior	Advantages of Changing	Disadvantages of Changing
• Likes the taste and the experience of drinking alcohol • Alcohol is a legal drug • Part of relaxing routine • Socially reinforced with coworkers	• Lessens concentration on daughter • Opens possibility of problems with police if driving intoxicated or if neighbors call the police • Could end up with a drinking problem • Exposing daughter to alcohol use habits	• Saves money by not buying as much wine • Eliminates risk of getting "in trouble" when police are called by antagonistic neighbor • Avoids future health problems associated with moderate daily drinking • Avoids future alcohol dependence • Has more attention span and time for playing with daughter at night	• Difficult going to sleep and changing bedtime ritual • Lost pleasure of tasting wine • Feel left out with coworkers when they are drinking wine • Difficult to cope with stress at the end of the day/relaxing

When talking about the exposure of her daughter to alcohol use, the mother decided that it would be better modeling if she did not drink during dinnertime when her daughter was around, but instead limited her drinking to after her daughter went to bed. Another goal that emerged from the decisional balance was that the client seemed to need to find other ways to relax after coming home from work and to fall asleep without depending on alcohol. This example illustrates that a decisional balance can lead to goal setting. Once a client identifies the needs that are being met by the problem behavior, these same needs can be targeted for healthier alternatives.

Another example is that of Jamaal, a 20-year-old black male residing at a residential youth independent living program. Jamaal's guidance counselor at the local community college referred Jamaal to the program because he no longer had a place to live. Jamaal reported that his mother suffers from alcoholism and that his older sister has bipolar disorder, and consequently both kicked him out of their homes. Jamaal has been attending school with a low C grade average. He has been working part-time at a local hardware store for over a year now as a cashier.

Recently, Jamaal has been living with two other males at the independent living program. Their apartment has been cited on several occasions by the program staff for filthy living conditions. Additionally, Jamaal reports that he has been spending most of his wages on food for himself and his roommates because his roommates are both unemployed. Staff members have told Jamaal on several occasions that he is not responsible for buying food for his roommates, but he continues to do so. When asked how he plans to broach the situation with his roommates, Jamaal plainly stated that he would prefer not to; that he has always had difficulties confronting others. See how the intern approaches the decisional balance technique with Jamaal.

Intern: So you are mad that no one cleans up after themselves, but you feel uncomfortable talking to your roommates. Can you tell me the advantages of not speaking to your roommates? I'm going to write them down.

Jamaal: Well, they aren't going to get mad at me.

Intern: So an advantage is that they'll like you.

Jamaal: I guess eventually someone else will bring up the mess and get the conversation going.

Intern: So another advantage is that maybe someone will step up and start the conversation.

Jamaal: (laughs) Maybe you guys will get so mad that you'll have a meeting and make us talk about it.

Intern: So another advantage is that if you don't communicate, the program will intervene. Anything else?

Jamaal: No, I can't think of anything else.

Intern: Now let's think of the disadvantages of not speaking to them.

Jamaal: I guess the biggest disadvantage is that I get stressed out when I come home.

> **Intern:** So not talking to them leads to stress.
>
> **Jamaal:** And the house will just stay messy and we might get bugs and stuff.
>
> **Intern:** So not talking to them could cause an infestation of roaches.
>
> **Jamaal:** And I am probably still going to get in trouble with you guys' cause you'll write us all up for the mess.
>
> **Intern:** So not talking to them may endanger your status in the program.
>
> **Jamaal:** Man, it sounds like something should happen now instead of later' cause I don't want to be kicked out.
>
> **Intern:** What do you think that something should be?
>
> **Jamaal:** I guess I have to talk to them' cause I can't wait that long. I already got one of those memo things from Ms. D.

Notice how Jamaal reaches his own conclusion that he needs to take action soon about the problem. He may not have reached the same point if the worker had simply told him what he needed to do. When he weighed the disadvantages compared to the advantages, the scale was tipped in favor of change.

EXERCISES

In the following situations, how would you use the technique of decisional balance?

> **Exercise 1:** The client, Richard, is a 48-year-old African American male who lives with his father. He has no source of income and lives only on the food that a faith-based agency provides him weekly. The intern at the agency has been working to help him find a job and referred him to the agency's Workforce Development Center to get help creating his résumé and sending it out.
>
> > **Richard:** Last time we met I referred you to our Workforce Development Center to get help with your résumé so you can send it out electronically to apply for multiple jobs. How did that go?
> >
> > **Richard:** I didn't go.
> >
> > **Intern:** What are some of the reasons you didn't go?
> >
> > **Richard:** I didn't want to.
> >
> > **Intern:** What are some of the reasons you don't want to go?
> >
> > **Richard:** I'm doing fine on my own about getting résumés out to people.
> >
> > **Intern:** How has that enabled you to get a job?
> >
> > **Richard:** It hasn't.
> >
> > **Intern:** How long have you been sending out résumés without getting a job?

Richard: Ten years.

Intern: What do you think would encourage you to get some assistance at the Workforce Development Center?

Richard: Nothing. I just don't want to go. There are no jobs available.

Exercise 2: Nadia is a 17-year-old girl in foster care who is currently failing all but one of her classes.

Intern: How are things at school?
Nadia: Fine.
Intern: Do you have a lot of work to do today?
Nadia: No.
Intern: Can you show me what you're working on in your classes?
Nadia: I didn't bring any of it home.
Intern: Okay, next time I'd like to see what you're working on.
Nadia: Okay, I'll try.
Intern: How have your grades been lately?
Nadia: I don't know. I still think Ds and Fs.
Intern: What can we do to improve your grades?
Nadia: I don't know.
Intern: How about your friend from math class? Could you two help each other?
Nadia: She's not very smart.
Intern: How about a tutor?
Nadia: Maybe, but I don't think so.

Exercise 3: Priya is a 17-year-old mother of a special-needs six-month-old girl.

Intern: Have you had a chance to meet some of the child care providers that live around your area?
Priya: No, I don't need a child care provider anymore.
Intern: Who is going to take care of your baby while you are at school?
Priya: I am not going back to school. I'd rather work.

Intern: What made you decide not to go back to school?

Priya: I am not good at school. I keep repeating the ninth grade. I'd rather work.

Intern: So you don't want to go back to school because you feel like you can't pass the ninth grade?

Priya: Yeah, school isn't for me; it just doesn't click in my head.

Intern: Well, Priya, don't forget that you were going through a lot while you were in school.

Priya: Yeah, but I just don't want to keep repeating the ninth grade. And I need to make money to pay for milk and other stuff for the baby.

Intern: Okay, but if you drop out of school, it is going to be very hard for you to go back . . . and expensive.

Priya: School isn't for me; I can work.

Exercise 4: Mrs. Hall is a 33-year-old African American single parent with three children, ages 15, 11, and 7. She had been receiving TANF (Temporary Assistance for Needy Families) assistance for the past three years since her husband deserted her. The intern writes, "During the past year, my agency made several efforts to get her a job, without success. The records showed that Mrs. Hall did not want to get a job, as she felt she was too busy taking care of her children, but the truth is that she is aware that getting a job will reduce her TANF check. I had the following conversation with her in other to motivate her to get a job."

Intern: What would you like to see yourself doing 10 years from now?

Mrs. Hall: I haven't given it much thought.

Intern: What about your current situation; how satisfied are you with it?

Mrs. Hall: I am not satisfied about my life now; it is very difficult to live on this inadequate TANF budget, to raise three children all by myself, and all the stress that comes from my husband deserting us.

Intern: I understand your concerns. It's true that past events have led to your current situation, but how you want your present and future to be will depend largely on you.

Mrs. Hall: How do you mean?

Intern: Take your financial situation for example; you have a choice between staying at home and seeking a job. If you don't begin to learn an employable skill now, and gradually work your way up in the job, what's going to happen in 10 years when you will no longer be eligible for the TANF payments?

Mrs. Hall: It would be nice to get a job, but there are also many reasons why it would not be possible for me to get a job.

Intern: Tell me more about that.

Mrs. Hall: Eventually, if I work, it would not add to my total income, because my TANF check will be reduced. I have also tried finding a job several times in the past and wasn't successful. I wouldn't be able to work and also take care of my home and family.

Intern: Having failed in the past doesn't mean you can't be successful this time. I hope you've heard the saying "if at first you don't succeed, try, try again," I encourage you to try again.

EXERCISE FOR YOUR PRACTICE

Are any of your clients afflicted with problem behaviors? If so, choose one that would be appropriate for the decisional balance technique. Write how you would introduce the technique to your client and how you would begin.

CONCLUSION

Taking a decisional balance to assess for problem behaviors allows clients to more clearly see all sides of their situation and helps motivate them to a more informed choice about what they must do. The decisional balance operationalizes the value of self-determination in which clients are allowed to have free choice in their life path (NASW, 1999). The decisional balance technique allows for self-determination because it is the client, rather than the social worker, who has to come to the conclusion about whether it is worth the effort to change a particular problem behavior. Having people explore the disadvantages as well as discussing the potential advantages of changing may lead to clients' own recognition that change is the path to take.

CHAPTER 6

EXPLORING THE SOLUTION

One of the themes of *Helping Skills for Social Work Direct Practice* is a focus on identifying and utilizing the strengths and resources that clients possess. From the initial process of engagement, you can begin to look for strengths and to work collaboratively. Social workers and other helping services professionals too often tend to evaluate clients based on pathology, e.g., what is wrong with clients and what they lack in their lives. This chapter emphasizes how to gather information about clients' strengths and how to help clients build upon them.

STRENGTHS-BASED QUESTIONS

We discussed in Chapter 3 the use of open-ended questions. In this chapter, we focus on the creation of strengths-based questions. They have three elements to them: 1) they are open-ended; 2) they imply that people are acting in their best interests and have the resources available to them ("What do your counselors and teachers do that is helpful for you?"); and 3) they use definitive phrasing.

Definitive words such as *when* and *will* imply that change *will* occur. For example, "*When* you are better, what *will* you be doing?" Use strengths-oriented questions to convey your certainty that change will occur. Contrast this to the tentative language of "*If* you feel better, what *could* you do?" The only occasion in which to use tentative language is when you talk about problems, as you do not want to presume that they will definitely occur. Instead, "*If* you feel frustrated, who can you talk to?" This question does not assume that the frustration will occur, but it does prepare the client for such an event.

Exercise: From the following list, circle the **open-ended questions**. Then put a star next to the **strengths-based questions**:

1.
   A. Tell me about what your child was doing during the argument.
   B. So where was your child during the argument?
   C. How did you keep your child safe during the argument?

2.
   A. Do you have any idea where you would like to work?
   B. What are your ideas about where you would like to work?
   C. What do you see yourself doing?

3.
   A. In what activities would you like to participate?
   B. What activities do you enjoy?
   C. Are there any activities in which you would like to participate?

4.
   A. How is your health?
   B. Tell me about your health.
   C. What do you do to take care of your health?

5.
   A. How do you keep your medications organized?
   B. Do you have any trouble organizing or taking your medication?
   C. How do you manage your medications?

6.
   A. So who's going to watch your child if you are going to work?
   B. What are your plans for your child while you are working?
   C. What ideas have you come up with for child care while you work?

7.
   A. What do you think your daughter hopes we'll accomplish through meeting together?
   B. What does your daughter want to be different as a result of our meeting?
   C. Why do you think your daughter would ask you to meet with me?

8.
   A. Tell me about any groups or organization in which you are involved.
   B. Are there groups or organizations here in which you are involved?
   C. In what groups and organizations here are you interested?

9.
   A. You told me that you had some questions for the foster dad.
   B. So, did you have a chance to ask questions and get answers from the dad?
   C. What happened with your plan to talk to the foster dad?

QUESTIONS THAT AMPLIFY STRENGTHS

There are other questions from solution-focused interviewing that may help your clients amplify their strengths:

- Questions about helpfulness:
  - "How is that helpful?"
  - "How was that helpful?"
  - "How will that be helpful?"
- Questions about difference:
  - "How did that make a difference?"
  - "How does that make a difference?"
  - "How will that make a difference?"

Note how the questions are phrased in different tenses to suit the occasion, but they are all generally used to get the client to identify his or her own solutions and resources. For instance, when Mariana, the 25-year-old immigrant from El Salvador, talks about scheduling another meeting with the doctor to get more information about cleft palate, the intern can ask, "How will that be helpful for you?" The client then articulates the benefits of this choice, making her more likely to follow through with it.

Another way in which the question can be used is when people have committed a positive action toward change. "How was that helpful for you?" allows them to savor the behavior they have taken, even if it is only a small step in the right direction. In this way, they have been reinforced for their choice and they see the reverberations of their actions. In the example above, after Mariana had the meeting with the doctor, the intern inquired, "How was that helpful for you?" Mariana, at that point, revealed that she had discovered that surgery could correct her child's cleft palate. She said, "There's still scars, but it's not that bad," signaling her beginning to come to terms with her unborn child's disability. She further seemed empowered to know that there was something she could do about the situation when she said, "Now that I know who the specialist is, I can call to set up the surgery."

The other way that the phrase "How is that helpful? can be used is to get a person to explore a problem behavior. For instance, Jen, a 17-year-old, has been admitted to an inpatient psychiatric hospital for a suicide attempt. She has been abusing drugs and alcohol and running away for days at a time. The clinical caseworker asked about the running away, "How was that helpful?" This is a nonconfrontational way of addressing negative behaviors while allowing the person to non-defensively explore what he or she is getting out of it.

STRENGTHS-BASED ASSESSMENT

Many books, courses, and agencies discuss assessment by focusing on a biopsychosocial assessment from the perspective of the problems in the client's life. This chapter focuses

---

EXHIBIT 6.1: Strengths-Based Assessment

Biological	Psychological	Spiritual	Social
• Health	• Coping		• Informal Social Support
	• Past Substance Abuse		• Formal Support
	• Suicide Risk		• Abuse (if relevant)
			• Employment
			• Parenting
			• School

---

instead on evaluating strengths and resources in the same domains that are typically covered in such an assessment. See Exhibit 6.1.

See Exhibit 6.2 for questions to use, and for a biopsychosocial-spiritual example, see Exhibit 6.3.

EXHIBIT 6.2: Strengths-Based Biopsychosocial-Spiritual Assessment

Biological

Health	What do you do to take care of your health?
Medication (if applicable)	How has your medication assisted you?
	How have you worked with the medication to make it help you?

Psychological

Coping (with the presenting problem)	What do you say to yourself that helps you cope?
	What do you do that helps?
	What spiritual resources do you draw upon?
	What supports do you draw upon?
	What financial or other physical resources do you have?
	What personal qualities do you use in this situation?
	What would others say you do that helps you cope?
Substance Abuse (if relevant)	How have you been able to stay sober or reduce your use (either current or in the past)?
	Who helped you and how did they help you? How might they be helpful to you again?
	If you experienced relapse, what signs indicated you were starting to slip? How would you bring things to an end?
	What can you do next time to be aware of these signs? What will you do when you see those signs?
	What have you learned from this experience?
History of Suicidality (if applicable)	If you have felt suicidal in the past, how were you able to get past that?
	What was helpful when you felt suicidal?
	What will it take to feel a little better now (if currently suicidal)?

Hobbies	What is something that you felt some pleasure or satisfaction in doing?
	Is this something that you do regularly now or did regularly in the past?
	What kinds of qualities, skills, or behaviors do you posses that allow you to do these things?
	What kinds of activities are you drawn to but haven't yet tried?

Social

Informal Social Support	When have others helped you?
	What did that person do that helped?
	How did you let that person know that you needed help?
	What do you think [_____] would say?
	How were you able to attract your romantic partner to you?
	What qualities and behaviors did your partner see in you that made him or her want to be with you?
	Which relationships have challenged you?
	How do/did you manage a challenging relationship?

Formal Support	What circumstances, situations, or feelings made you decide to seek services?
	What have you found helpful about any professional help you've received?
	What did you find least helpful about the experience?

Abuse (if relevant)	Think of a time when you were in an abusive situation and were threatened but managed to escape or avoid harm, even if just temporarily. How did you do that?
	If you were able to leave an abusive situation in the past, how were you able to leave?
	What did you do in that situation?
	What did you say to yourself?
	How were you able to seek help from others or gain support?
	What qualities in yourself did you draw on?
	What resources did you draw upon to survive the situation?
	How did you decide to behave differently than those who hurt you?

Employment	How did you sell yourself in your résumé and job interview that allowed you to get the job?
	What did you tell your current or most recent employer that might have contributed to your being hired?
	Think of a recent situation, or one that stands out in your mind, at work when you were proud of the way you handled something. What did you do?
	What did you say to yourself?
	What do you think your boss, coworkers, or customers thought about you in that situation?
	What did others who know how you handled this situation say about you?
	Think of a recent difficult situation in your job or one that stands out in your mind. How did you meet, or work toward meeting, that challenge?
	What goals do you have related to your career or job?

Parenting	What do you think your children would say makes you a good parent?
	When do you think you are your best as a parent?
	Describe a situation in which you were proud of your parenting.
	What did you do?
	What did you say to your children?
	How did your children react to you?
	When is a time that you have enjoyed your children?
	What did you do?
	What did you say to them?
	What qualities, behaviors, beliefs, and supports have you drawn on as a parent?
	What qualities, behaviors, beliefs, and supports have you developed as a parent?
	How have you decided to behave differently from your own parents?
	How have you made that happen?
School	How did you manage to make it through (6th grade, high school, trade school, junior college, a four-year university, two years of college, graduate school, etc.)?
	What qualities do you posses that made that happen?
	What did you find most challenging about school?
	How did you manage any difficulties that you may have encountered while in school (e.g., completing homework assignments, tests, getting to school on time, moving from one grade to another, teacher/classmates relationships, sports)?
	In what ways did school prepare you for future challenges?
Culture (if from non-mainstream culture)	What values in your culture do you take pride in?
	Who are the role models in your community? Why?
	How do you instill cultural knowledge and pride in your children?
	What places in your community help foster a sense of community and positive identity?
Spiritual	
	What spiritual beliefs help you cope with difficulties?
	How does attending religious services or engaging in religious practices fulfill you in a spiritual sense?
	What spiritual practices do you follow? How do these help?
	What meaning do you make of the challenges you've faced?
	What are the benefits of having gone through this experience?

EXHIBIT 6.3: Biopsychosocial-Spiritual Assessment Sample

Introduction

Olga is a 43-year-old mother of two who has been diagnosed with diabetes, hepatitis C, cirrhosis of the liver, and neuropathy. Olga's liver is currently not functional, and her chances of obtaining a liver transplant are slim because she lacks health insurance. Olga is currently required to go to the hospital on a weekly basis to receive paracentesis (removal of fluid from the abdominal cavity). The fluid in her abdomen has resulted in excessive weight gain. Olga has difficulty walking distances greater than 10 feet. Olga's illness has meant that her children, who are ages 9 and 10, have had to take on more responsibilities around the house. Both children have noticed a change in their mother, although she has not revealed to them the true nature of her illness.

Biological

Olga says she takes care of herself by eating right (lots of vegetables and fruits). She also makes herself get out of bed each day to do some sort of movement, even if it is just to walk to the kitchen and back. She keeps her mind sharp by watching educational programs, reading, and interacting with her children.

She believes that some of her medication helps her and that some doesn't. She has not talked to her doctors about this, and she says, "I just take more, or cut down, based on how I am feeling and what my body needs."

Psychological

Coping

Olga copes with her illness by talking positively to herself, saying, "I can do it. I must do it." She uses her sense of humor and optimism ("If life gives you lemons, make lemonade"). She draws heavily on her spirituality, her belief in God, and she prays a lot. When she was asked what others would say that helps her cope, she responded, "They would say I do the best with what I got."

Olga has a substance use history, but states a conviction not to relapse: "Life is too short and my children are too precious to me. I want to be able to watch my children grow up and to teach them right from wrong. I don't want to hurt my chances of being considered for a liver transplant. Spiritually, I want to do the right thing because I want to end up where I want to end up, heaven."

Hobbies

When asked, "What is something that you felt some pleasure or satisfaction in doing?" Olga answered, "Before I got sick, I enjoyed singing, swimming, dancing. Now I enjoy just being able to get out and interact with others since I am stuck in this house most of the time. I love being able to ride my scooter to the store, or take the kids to the park and just watch them play. Also, I guess I could still sing."

Social

Informal Social Support

Olga identified her family as a support. Her mother helps with cleaning the house, picking up groceries, and other errands. Olga's children fetch items for her and help out with chores around the house. She said she was able to reach out and ask for the help she received when she became sick, seeing that she "didn't have much choice then."

She identified relationships with her parents as those who have challenged her. She stated that she managed these relationship difficulties by learning to be assertive and by speaking up for herself.

Formal Support

When Olga was a teenager she ran away from home to get away from the abuse she suffered from her parents. She drew on several qualities within herself to make this happen, including a strong will to escape the abuse and the courage to change her situation. At the time, Olga stayed at a runaway shelter, where she talked to counselors. She said it was also beneficial to be with other teens who lived through similar situations.

Employment

Olga says she can no longer work because of her illness, but that she had gotten jobs in the past because of her "reputation and experience." "I would tell the owner, 'Let me take care of you, and I would give them a facial,' and I always got hired because I was good."

Parenting

Olga reflected on her experiences as a parent. When asked, "What do you think your children would say makes you a good parent?" she said, "I hope they would say that they can talk to me about anything and that I make good on my promises." Responding to the question, "When do you think you're able to be your best as a parent?" Olga says, "Honestly, I think I'm a better parent now than before I was sick. I am able to spend more quality time with my children. Although we can't go places, I think just being with them and talking with them is important. I never did that much before; I was more work oriented." She said that she is proud of her parenting when she sees her children "doing better" or dealing with a situation differently after talking about why it was important they change their behavior and discussing the benefits of doing so. Olga mentioned that she enjoys her children "when they do things they didn't think they could do, or didn't have faith in themselves to try originally."

Olga identified that she looks to God for help ("He always knows what you're doing") and for the patience to be a good parent. Parenting has increased her level of patience and her belief that "Sometimes you just have to let things happen. You can't control everything about your children. Sometimes you have to let them figure it out for themselves."

When asked, "How have you decided to behave differently from your own parents?" Olga said, "Be there for my children. Show them I love them and tell them I love them. I tell them what they did wrong, why they are getting a consequence. Talk to them about right and wrong. Not put them down for being who they are, but encourage them to be who they are and be proud of that."

School

Olga reports that school was difficult for her because she was bullied by her classmates, but then she became more assertive in high school. Getting her high school diploma was important to her, so she obtained her GED.

Culture

Olga stated that her African American cultural group values include "being on time, having a work ethic, and doing the right thing." Although she said she didn't have any role models growing up, she instills pride in her children by "telling them where they're from and to not be ashamed of who they are." She identified her church as a place that fosters a sense of community and positive cultural identity

Spirituality

Olga says her belief in God "helps me know that despite what I'm going through, everything will be fine, because He has a plan for me. I can't change the plan, but there is one, so I just leave it up to God. This helps take all my anxiety away." Going to church gives her hope and allows her to interact with other people. When asked about the meaning she makes of the challenges she's faced, she states, "I believe that the closer you are to God, the more the devil tries to push you down. The pain and struggles I face are the devil trying to take my soul. It's a test of my faith to God. Through this experience, it makes me stronger, physically, mentally, and spiritually. It brings me closer to God."

She says she has experienced benefits from her illness in that it has made her a stronger person: "What doesn't kill me makes me stronger." She says it has also helped her identify who her true friends are, and what love from her family means when she has gone through low points in her disease.

Summary: Assessment

You will note that when you complete a strengths-based assessment, you are able to draw a more complete picture of the client—he or she has become a real person rather than just a list of problems. The process of completing the assessment assists both the worker and the client to more fully appreciate the strengths and resources the client brings, and the client is more empowered as a result. When people are empowered, they are better able to meet their challenges and to problem-solve.

In particular, the questions helped the intern working in a family preservation program to understand the role that Olga's spirituality and faith played in her ability to cope with her illness and the subsequent limitations. By allowing her to talk about her faith and the meaning she ascribes to her experiences, the intern helped her place her current struggles into the context of her life and her belief system. The intern was concerned that Olga's children did not know the extent of their mother's illness, and that they had not discussed this as a family. But when Olga spontaneously mentioned that "she could talk to her children about anything," this gave the intern a lead-in to introduce a family discussion about the mother's illness.

Additionally, the assessment revealed that Olga has good self-awareness. She is able to verbalize a sense of personal accomplishment when she says that she "always got hired" because she was good. She noted her sense of humor and her optimism as qualities that bring her through difficulties. Her statements about herself reveal self-confidence and an internal motivation to "do the right thing." The intern can use this to talk to her about the fact that she is self-regulating her medication, and perhaps have a discussion about whether this is the best approach.

Olga's children are a real source of pride and motivation for her. She has a desire to be different with them than her parents were with her. The intern can focus on this to discuss some specific ways to do this, given the limitations of her current illness. She has strong motivation to stay away from addictive substances, and this comes from a number of assessment areas: spiritual (wants to please God and go to heaven), parenting (wants to be there for her children), biological (wants to receive a new liver). The intern can reinforce this decision.

EXERCISES

MULTIPLE-CHOICE QUESTIONS

1. Client is a 14-year-old, Latino male in a gang prevention program. He hands the social worker his behavior chart from school for the week. The social worker responds, "A lot of 2s—very good. What happened here? I see a 1 on Monday, and another 1 here that says 'needs notebook.'"
   The following are optimal strengths-oriented questions EXCEPT:
   A. What are some things you could do so that you don't receive a 1 in that class anymore?
   B. What do you need to do to receive a 2 in that class?
   C. What does your teacher need to see to give you a 2 in that class?
   D. What have you been doing to get all these 2s?

2. Continuing with the client from 1 above, **what are strengths-based ways to encourage accountability of the client?**
   Social worker: And what about this 1, from fifth period?
   Client: I left class before the bell. The teacher was yelling at me for no reason.
   A. Simple reflection: You left the class before the bell.
   B. Relationship question: What would the teacher say is the reason?

C. Closed-ended question: Do you think maybe there was a reason?
D. A and B

3. At a health clinic for low-income women, an intern shadows a social worker seeing a 20-year-old woman from Ghana who is 14 weeks pregnant and HIV positive. After asking for her name and birth date, the social worker proceeds as follows:

Social worker: We need to ask you some very personal questions. Is it okay with you?
Client: Yes.
Social worker: How old were you when you first had intercourse?
Client laughs nervously.
Social worker: How old were you when you had sex for the first time?
Client: 15.
Social worker: How many sex partners have you had?
Client is quiet.
Social worker: You are 20 now, so how many sex partners have you had in five years?
Client: Four, three.
Social worker: Three or four?
Client: Three.
Social worker: So you have had three partners in five years?
Client: Yes.
Social worker: What was the highest grade you completed?
Client: I went to school for 10 years.
Social worker: Do you take any medication?
Client: Kaletra and Truvada.
Social worker: What doses?
Client: I don't know.
Social worker: Here is a package of information you may need. We have breast-feeding classes.
Client: I will not breastfeed because I am HIV positive.
Social worker: We also have birth control classes. Do you use birth control?
Client: Yes, Depo-Provera and condoms.
Social worker: You need to get a car seat for the baby when he or she is born. You also need to find a pediatrician before you deliver.

The following are strengths-based questions that could be used instead of the above dialogue EXCEPT:

    A. Tell me about your medication.
    B. How do you take care of your health?
    C. How have you been able to get control of the HIV?
    D. What have you learned about HIV that you have been able to apply to yourself?

SHORT ANSWER QUESTIONS

Exercise 1: In the following scenario, the social worker compliments the client, Maharene, a 35-year-old Ethiopian female, on what she has accomplished. The client came to the United States three years ago under the assumption of having a good job in place. However, she was trafficked, sold into domestic servitude, and kept as a slave. She escaped after one year and soon after came to an apartment transition program. Maharene struggles with the fear of running into the people who trafficked her. Therefore, she isolates herself in her apartment and will leave only to go to work, the grocery store, or the program for classes. Even though she is religious and very lonely, she will not participate in Ethiopian church services. In fact, she is particularly adverse to the Ethiopian community because her traffickers were Ethiopian. What solution-focused, open-ended questions could be asked to identify additional resources?

Intern: How have you been doing?
Maharene: Good.
Intern: You are now working full-time, which is very good. And you will soon be graduating from our program.
Maharene: Yes, and I get compliments from the customers.
Intern: That is great! What have you been doing to find an apartment?
Maharene: Yes, but I have not found anything that I can afford.
Intern: Maybe you should look for a basement apartment in a house.
Maharene: No, that bothers my head.
Intern: Why does it bother your head?
Maharene: It is dark. No windows.
Intern: You do not like basement apartments because they are dark and depressing.
Maharene: Yes, yes, depressing.
Intern: I see.
Maharene: Sometimes I call places, but they cannot understand my English.
Intern: Do you have a friend who can help you make phone calls while looking for an apartment?
Maharene: Yes, but she is always working when I am off.
Intern: Do you have anyone else that might be able to help you make phone calls and set up appointments?
Maharene: (She bursts into tears) No, I do not have anybody here. My family is all in Ethiopia.
Intern: Let's sit down.
Maharene: I am sorry.
Intern: It is okay. Anyone in your situation would feel this way. I know you are Christian; do you belong to a church here?
Maharene: No, I cannot understand them.

Intern: A church might be a good way for you to meet some good people, even if you do not understand every word they say. You have accomplished a lot in the two years that you have been in our program. You now have full-time work and are able to speak some English. You are continuing to take ESL classes to further improve your English skills, and you are meeting with an attorney to get your children. We are going to help you through this transition.

Exercise 2: In the following scenario, what areas could you explore further with strengths-based questions?

Calvin is a 30-year-old African American male diagnosed with bipolar disorder. He identifies himself as gay and is currently homeless and living with different friends in the area.

Intern: Hello, what brings you in today?

Calvin: Well, um, I was hospitalized a couple of weeks ago. I had like a breakdown cuz I've been going through so much, so I just finally broke down. Someone in the hospital told me about you guys and suggested that I come here.

Intern: Ok. Well I'm happy that you came here. What do you think caused your breakdown?

Calvin: Oh my goodness. So much has gone on in the past couple of years. I don't know where to start. I guess it happened because I'm homeless right now. I lost my job, lost my apartment. I went through a really bad breakup and I just have a lot of past issues going on.

Intern: Wow, it seems as though you have a lot of tough issues to deal with right now.

Calvin: Yeah, I really do. Plus I don't have any really supportive people in my life. I mean, I've been through stuff before and I had good friends to count on so I got through it, but now I just have me.

Intern: You're probably feeling that you can't handle this all on your own?

Calvin: Definitely.

Intern: So to start the intake I have to ask some questions about your family history. Are you okay discussing that?

Calvin: Sure. It's crazy but I can talk about it.

Intern: Tell me about your childhood. Where did you grow up?

Calvin: I was born in Montgomery County, MD, but raised in DC. Um, in a nutshell, my dad killed my mom at 14 and then killed himself. After that, it was all downhill. I got emancipated at 16 and moved to New York. I've pretty much been on my own ever since.

Intern: Wow. I can only imagine the pain you felt from losing both your parents, and especially in the way that it happened. It was probably a very emotional time for you.

Calvin: Well, not really. At the time I was so young I don't think I really processed it the right way. I turned to doing a lot of grown-up things that I had no business doing, but they made me feel better.

Intern: So when you say, "grown up things," what do you mean exactly?

Calvin: Well, I started using marijuana. And I was sexually molested at 14 by a male relative, so after that I started experimenting with all kinds of drugs. I also realized that I was gay around that age too, so a lot was going on.

Intern: Yes, it definitely seems like there was. Do you mind clarifying how you realized you were gay at that age?

Calvin: Well, I just identified with that culture after I was molested. That had something to do with it, but not all of it. I just loved to dance, and that community really accepted me when I moved to New York. I mean, I was a 16-year-old, hanging out with people that were older, but they embraced me.

Intern: Is your sexual orientation something you're comfortable with?

Calvin: Definitely. I have straight friends, gay friends, I'm comfortable with me. I'm just not comfortable with dating right now.

Intern: Okay. So you mentioned that you experimented with different drugs. Do you mind naming those?

Calvin: PCP, ecstasy, alcohol, lots of pills, some things I didn't even know about. Mainly I used drugs from age 17–21. I did so many drugs that after age 21 I had no desire to drink or do any of that because I had done so much when I lived in New York. When I finally came back to DC, I think I was burnt out.

Intern: Can you explain how you were burnt out?

Calvin: I went through a horrible dating relationship, and then with all the drugs I had been using I was just a mess. I came back to DC, though, at 21 and just really got back on my feet.

Intern: How so?

Calvin: Well, I got a job and started building my business.

Intern: What kind of work did you do?

Calvin: Well in New York I was a trained dancer, so I did some music videos and even a dance show on TV. But my passion was cooking. I came to DC and became a chef. I'm a trained vegan chef and a waiter. I made a lot of money working at some of the best restaurants in DC.

Intern: So what happened to your last job?

Calvin: I can't keep a job to save my life. I've had like 35 jobs and gotten fired from almost all of them. I don't know, I guess I just don't take no mess. I just can't have people talking to me any kind of way.

Intern: Well, it seems as if it's easy for you to get jobs, and you have an impressive work history. But you have a problem with authority?

Calvin: Yeah, I guess. I just feel that I'm so talented. I mean, I've won awards at jobs and raises because I've been such a good waiter. But management hates me. Sometimes I think it's because I work at mostly Caucasian establishments in the most expensive part of town and I'm black and gay.

Intern: You just said a lot there. Explain more about how you feel about being a black gay man.

Calvin: I could talk about this for hours. I just feel that when people look at me they think one thing, but what they don't know is that I'm highly intelligent. My parents were very smart people, with money. I'm a classically trained dancer, musician, and chef. I have a lot of talents. But I'm obviously black and gay, and sometimes people only take me for those two things.

Intern: Basically, you believe that there are many parts to you. You're intelligent, you are musically inclined, and you can cook. However, you think that the only things people notice about you are that you're black and gay.

Calvin: Yes. It bothers me, but I know that I'm not the only person going through this. That's why I want to work for myself because I don't have to worry about management questioning my skills. Customers love me, but for some reason my bosses were always hating on me.

Intern: Is that an area of your life you would like help with?

Calvin: Yes, I need another job until I can get my business on track; that's why I'm homeless now.

Intern: What happened to your apartment?

Calvin: Well, I have really bad credit. I can always find someone to help me get the apartment, but I don't know how to save money and pay my bills, so I end up losing the apartment because of that.

Intern: Well, it seems as though you're pretty irresponsible with your money. Where are you staying now?

Calvin: With friends. I hate it there, though; they treat me as if I'm nothing.

Intern: Why do you think they do that?

Calvin: Because I lost my job and place. But what they don't realize is that it could happen to anyone. I'm going to change my life, though.

Intern: You seem pretty hopeful that you'll get out of this situation. I understand that you've been homeless and jobless before. How do you plan to succeed this time?

Calvin: Well, I guess I'm starting by coming here. I've never asked for help before, like from an agency. I heard you guys help with housing, so that would be great. I need a lot of therapy too. I've already started working on my business making vegan meals for clients. I'm hopeful.

Intern: Well, it seems as though you're hopeful about your situation, and you've shown that by reaching out to us for help. We can set some treatment goals for you to work on with your case manager, and try to work with you to become more independent. Thank you for being so open and for coming in today.

Exercise 3: In this section of an intake for a woman being admitted into a halfway house after leaving a prison setting, the caseworker in this portion of the interview centered mainly on questions having to do with the client's physical health. How would you go about asking these questions from a strengths-based perspective?

Caseworker: I have some questions regarding your health and the goals you would like to set for your time at the Guest House. Some of these medical questions may sound familiar because you were asked them on your application. But we need to ask them again when you enter the house. Do you have any medical, mental health or dental problems now?

Resident: No.

Caseworker: Have you ever been told that you have a chronic disease or other serious medical problem that needs monitoring?

Resident: Depression.

Caseworker: Have you ever taken medication?

Resident: Yes, several over the years.

Caseworker: What kinds?

Resident: Wellbutrin, Zoloft, a couple more, but—

Caseworker: All at the same time?

Resident: No, when one didn't work I would try another.

Caseworker: Any now?

Resident: No.

Caseworker: So why did you stop taking them?

Resident: I felt like I didn't need them, I gained a lot of weight and I felt like they made me more depressed. I started in middle school and didn't do any of the things that kids my age did, and I wanted to be more like them.

Caseworker: Do you have any allergies to food or medication?

Resident: No.

Caseworker: Do you smoke cigarettes?

Resident: Yes, but I'm trying to quit.

Caseworker: You were just in [prison], and you couldn't smoke there. What happened?

Resident: I just picked it up, but after this pack I'm going to stop.

Caseworker: That's good because we are going to be a nonsmoking facility soon, so you will have to stop. We will be hosting a lot of speakers and classes at the house about smoking to help the residents quit. I know how painful it can be.

Have you ever used alcohol or street drugs?

Resident: Yes.

Caseworker: When did you start?

Resident: I tried pot at 16 and crack at 23. Also did liquor.

Caseworker: Do you need to see a doctor?

Resident: No.
Caseworker: When was your last physical?
Resident: March.
Caseworker: In [prison]?
Resident: Yes.
Caseworker: Could any of the following risk factors for HIV infection apply to you? Blood transfusion since 1986?
Resident: No.
Caseworker: Shooting drugs ever in the past?
Resident: No.
Caseworker: Many different male sex partners in the past?
Resident: No.
Caseworker: Sex partner ever shot drugs?
Resident: No.
Caseworker: You sure?
Resident: Yes.
Caseworker: Male sex partner ever had sex with another man?
Resident: I've suspected, but I'm not sure.
Caseworker: You might be right. Have you ever been tested?
Resident: Yes.
Caseworker: When was your most recent test?
Resident: When I had my last physical.

Here is the following dialogue once again with some strengths-based questions that are designed as alternative responses (in bold). How would this have made a difference in terms of rapport and empowerment of the client?

Caseworker: I have some questions regarding your health and the goals you would like to set for your time at the Guest House. Do you have any medical, mental health, or dental problems now?
[What is your health like now?]
Resident: No.
Caseworker: Have you ever been told that you have a chronic disease or other serious medical problem that needs monitoring?
Resident: Depression.
Caseworker: Have you ever taken medication?
[What treatment have you received? What was helpful? What was not so helpful?]
Resident: Yes, several over the years.
Caseworker: What kinds?
Resident: Wellbutrin, Zoloft, a couple more, but—
Caseworker: All at the same time?
Resident: No, when one didn't work I would try another.

Caseworker: Any now?

Resident: No.

Caseworker: So why did you stop taking them?

Resident: I felt like I didn't need them. I gained a lot of weight and I felt like they made me more depressed. I started in middle school and didn't do any of the things that kids my age did, and I wanted to be more like them.

[**How were you able to get past the depression?**]

Caseworker: Do you have any allergies to food or medication?

Resident: No.

Caseworker: Do you smoke cigarettes?

Resident: Yes, but I'm trying to quit.

Caseworker: You were just in [prison], and you couldn't smoke there. What happened?

[**How were you able to keep the cravings from taking over at (prison)?**]

Resident: I just picked it up, but after this pack I'm going to stop.

Caseworker: That's good because we are going to be a nonsmoking facility soon, so you will have to stop. We will be hosting a lot of speakers and classes at the house about smoking to help the residents quit. I know how painful it can be.

Have you ever used alcohol or street drugs?

[**What has been your experience with alcohol or street drugs?**]

Resident: Yes.

Caseworker: When did you start?

Resident: I tried pot at 16 and crack at 23. Also did liquor.

Caseworker: Do you need to see a doctor?

Resident: No.

Caseworker: When was your last physical?

Resident: March.

Caseworker: In [prison]?

Resident: Yes.

Caseworker: Could any of the following risk factors for HIV infection apply to you? Blood transfusion since 1986?

[**What do you know about risk factors for HIV and how they apply to you?**]

Resident: No.

Caseworker: Shooting drugs ever in the past?

Resident: No.

Caseworker: Many different male sex partners in the past?

Resident: No.

Caseworker: Sex partner ever shot drugs?

Resident: No.

Caseworker: You sure?

Resident: Yes.

> **Caseworker:** Male sex partner ever had sex with another man?
> **Resident:** I've suspected but I'm not sure.
> **Caseworker:** You might be right. Have you ever been tested?
> [**When was your most recent HIV test?**]

This discussion and the accompanying examples and exercises show how typical biopsychosocial assessments can be enlarged upon by the addition of strengths-based questions. In this way, you obtain a more balanced assessment of the client—both their problems and their strengths. As a result, you will see clients in a more holistic fashion and as real persons rather than clients who are riddled with problems. You can also use the strengths you have helped them identify as a springboard for problem solving.

EXERCISES FOR YOUR PRACTICE

Exercise 1: Think about the "difficult" client you discussed in Chapter 2. After reading the previous material, come up with at least three additional strengths than you were able to compliment in Chapter 2's exercise.

Exercise 2: If your agency has a typical intake or biopsychosocial assessment form, consider what questions you would add, take away, or change to make the assessment a more balanced appraisal between problems and strengths.

EXCEPTION FINDING

A key intervention technique in solution-focused interviewing is delving into the details of exceptions, defined as times when the problem does not occur (de Jong & Berg, 2008). The purpose of exception finding is to help people access and expand upon the resources and strengths they use to combat difficulties. Helping individuals find abilities and behaviors that have served them well in the past is easier than teaching them entirely new ones (Bertolino & O'Hanlon, 2002). Exception finding also reduces the dichotomous thinking that often afflicts people when they are so embroiled in their problems that they cannot see the gray areas, only the black and white. Identifying exceptions thus helps people shrink the all-encompassing nature of their problems and allows them to see their problems as much more fluid and changeable.

Steps for exception finding are as follows:

1. Identify a problem (example: running away).
2. Ask what the person would like to see instead of the problem in terms of the presence of positive behaviors (example: staying at home).
3. Ask about when this positive behavior occurred.
4. If a client is unable to come up with exceptions, ask about "when things are a little better" (example: if teen runs every day, ask about the times of day she is at home or when she gets back earlier).
5. Help the client figure out what makes the exception happen (see Exhibit 6.4).
6. Help the client figure out how to enlarge on the exception and/or apply it to the problem.

These steps will be applied to a variety of examples drawn from different social work settings. Some of the potential pitfalls in using exception finding are laid out in Exhibit 6.5.

EXHIBIT 6.4: **Exceptions**

Question	Solution
When?	
What's the typical timing (time of day, week, month, or year) when you feel better?	
How often do you experience exceptions to depression (once an hour, once a day, once a week)?	
How long do they last?	
Where?	
Where are you when you feel best?	
What is it about the setting that helps you feel better?	
What?	
What bodily reactions have you experienced when you've felt better?	
What actions do you take to make the exception happen?	
What do you tell yourself when this happens?	
Who?	
Who contributes to your feeling better?	
What do they do that helps?	

EXHIBIT 6.5: Exception Finding: Pitfalls and Solutions

Pitfalls	Solutions
Finding exceptions too early in the process before a family feels understood for the problem	Listen and reflect feelings; Use coping questions
Process is abandoned too quickly when client is unable to come up with an exception.	Inquire about when a problem is less intense, frequent, or severe; Ask a relationship question about what others would see as an exception; If all else fails, ask the client what he/she is doing to prevent the problem from becoming worse.
Failing to elicit details of the exception	Use the investigative questions (who, what, where, when, how) to elicit contextual details of the exception.
Not applying solutions to problem situations	Spend sufficient time on the exception so that clients begin to feel more successful and able to invoke further change; Ask clients how they can use their strengths to help them with their problems; Role-play to try out skills in different situations; Identify where there are gaps in knowledge and skills and work with the client to correct these.
Clients attribute exceptions to events ("the sun was shining") and people ("she was just acting nice") other than to their own efforts.	Ask questions about what they were doing differently when "the sun was shining"/"she was just acting nice."

Berg (1994); Christensen et al. (1999)

Example 1: Grace is a 40-year-old Caucasian woman diagnosed with schizoaffective disorder. When the social work intern asked what made things a little bit better, she said, "When things are really hard I like to take time out to rest and relax. I may lie down in my bed or just concentrate on tuning out the voices in my head. When I take a break to rest, I feel better, calmer." When asked to elaborate more on how this exception makes a difference, Grace reports that she has more energy to interact with others and carry out tasks when she is able to take a "time-out" during the day. The social work intern then asked how she can ensure that the client gets this quiet time when she needs it, as Grace lives with roommates who are often present in the house. Grace decided to set aside a certain amount of time each day to go to her room and spend time alone to relax for 30 minutes.

In this example, Grace identified an activity she can do that helps her cope, and the intern worked with her to encourage this activity on a daily basis.

Example 2: Kim is a 37-year-old Caucasian female who entered a county detox center to withdraw from alcohol and cocaine. She has a 14-year-old son who is currently in the custody of her ex-husband. Kim has a job waiting for her after she completes the 90-day treatment program that follows detox. Kim has been to treatment in the past, under court order, but admits that she wasn't interested in becoming sober then. She reports that she now wants to get clean and take treatment seriously.

Intern: Have you ever done this before?

Kim: Yes, a long time ago.

Intern: How were you able to get clean that time?

Kim: I don't know.

Intern: In the past, how have you been able to work and raise your son without drinking or using cocaine?

Kim: Well, when I would get stressed out or angry I would go to an AA meeting. That support system really helped me a lot.

Intern: How did you know to go to an AA meeting when you were that frustrated and annoyed?

Kim: I told myself that if I didn't go to a meeting and talk about my desire to use that I was going to get a drink and lose my son.

Intern: That was a good choice you made, very smart thinking. Are meetings something you think would help you again?

Kim: I think they can, but I'll need to go more often and not just when I'm about to drink.

Intern: So what you're saying is that you find meetings helpful in maintaining your sobriety, and you recognize that going more often will help keep you sober. Going more often will be better than going only when you feel that you're about to drink.

In this situation, the intern was able to help her client identify what was helpful during a previous period of abstinence. The client went on to name how she could use this exception even more effectively in the future.

Example 3: Cheryl is the mother of Ryan, a 14-year-old African American male who has recently returned to live with his mother and sister after living in a residential facility for two and a half years. The intern is working with Ryan through home-based services.

Intern: Tell me about a time when Ryan talks in a normal tone of voice.

Cheryl: He does that on the weekdays, but not on the weekends.

Intern: What's different about the weekdays?

Cheryl: We have more structure during the weekdays.

Intern: And what does that look like?

Cheryl: I work and he goes to school and has his therapy sessions, and then we have dinner, watch TV, and go to bed.

Cheryl: So what could happen on the weekend to make things more like what is going on in the week that keeps your son calm?

Cheryl: We need to make a routine, similar to what's going on during the week.

Intern: Let's break that down. What would the routine look like?

Cheryl: Well, during the week he gets up at 6:00 a.m., takes a shower, eats breakfast, and is picked up to go to school by 7:00 a.m. On the weekends he gets up whenever he wants to, although it's rarely past 9 a.m., but I'd like to just have him continue to get up at 6 a.m., take his shower, and eat breakfast to keep the routine of the weekday.

Intern: That sounds like a great idea. Since there is no school during the weekend, what else will he be doing?

Cheryl: One of his counselors comes over to pick him up, usually in the afternoon around 12 p.m. They're gone for about three or four hours.

Intern: So the afternoon is taken care of. By the time he comes home from seeing his counselors, it's just about the time he would be returning from school. So, what can you do in the morning after shower and breakfast to create more structure?

Cheryl: I can allot him a certain amount of time to watch some cartoons, because it is the weekend, and then I can take him to the Boys and Girls Club. They open at 8:30 a.m. on weekends, and they're only a 10-minute drive from my house.

Intern: And let's say that the Boys and Girls Club is closed one weekend and you're not able to take him there for the four hours before his counselor would come over to pick him up. How would you create some structure during that time?

Cheryl: Hmmm. There are always chores around the house, and I know he always has some homework to do. Usually he does his homework with his counselors, but he could do some of it at home instead. As far as chores, there is always laundry to do, dusting and mopping, stuff like that.

Intern: How would you get him to work on these things?

Cheryl: I used to have a schedule with chores listed throughout the week, and my daughter and son were assigned different tasks around the house. But a couple of years ago I just got so busy with work and life that I didn't keep up with it. I need to remake that schedule and post it on the fridge. Then he'll have chores to do for a couple of hours on the weekends.

Intern: So, to clarify, Ryan will get up at 6:00 a.m., take a shower, eat breakfast, and watch some cartoons until when?

Cheryl: Let's say 8:00 a.m.

Intern: Then, at 8:00 a.m., he will begin chores for two hours until 10:00 a.m.

Cheryl: That sounds about right. And then he can start on any homework he has for the next hour. Then, at 11:00 a.m., I can make him lunch and he can relax until his counselor arrives around noon.

Intern: That sounds like a great plan. Very detailed. So, the only time left to reexamine is weekend evenings. What time do you normally have dinner, watch TV, and go to bed during the weekday?

Cheryl: We eat dinner around 6:30 p.m., and then he watches TV until he has to go to bed at 9 p.m. Instead of me allowing him to stay up until 10 p.m. or 11 p.m. on Fridays and Saturdays, I will keep his bedtime at 9 p.m. to maintain the routine.

Intern: These sound like excellent solutions to maintain what has been working right for you during the week.

This exchange allows the intern and the client to explore in detail what their lives look like when her son is behaving well and to replicate this plan on the weekend when their relationship is currently problematic. The client seems hopeful that the problem will improve and by the end of the meeting appears much less overwhelmed.

Example 4: Sean is an 18-year-old Caucasian, gay male who is dealing with an emotional cutoff from his parents after he revealed his sexual orientation. Recently he was unemployed and homeless, but has since found employment and housing. He is currently seeking case management through the homeless and low-income drop-in program, where he comes for some of his meals. Sean starts the following interchange by talking about how he feels hatred toward himself, and the intern begins the process of exception finding.

Intern: Think about the last time you felt a little better about yourself. Tell me about that time.

Sean: I think I got one. It was about a month ago.

Intern: What was different about that time?

Sean: I felt strong. I felt good about myself.

Intern: What was happening during this time?

Sean: Well, I was at work and I had this really difficult table—a very demanding party of eight. They were there throughout my shift and kept running me. It seemed like they were never satisfied with anything. But, at the end of the evening, one of the party members came up to me and told me how notorious they were for running their waiters around and said that I did an excellent job and handed me a 40% tip.

Intern: That's pretty amazing. Those kinds of tables must be daunting! What qualities did you draw on to deal with that situation?

Sean: I think I'm pretty good at organization and multitasking. You really have to be to be a good waiter. And I want to be a good waiter, so I pushed myself to keep moving. I guess part of it was my stubbornness too. I told myself that I would show them just how good I was!

Intern: So, how did you feel afterward?

Sean: I felt great. I felt like I had really accomplished something. And that made me feel good about me. I was proud of myself.

Intern: How often does this happen at your job?

Sean: Well, now that I think about it, I guess I feel that way a couple of times a week.

Intern: And what is it about those times that helps you feel good about yourself?

Sean: Similar things, I guess, like feeling a sense of accomplishment from knowing that I worked hard. And sometimes my boss notices how hard I've been working and tells me that I've done a good job. That always feels good.

Intern: So, Sean, from what you've said it sounds like what makes you feel good about yourself is working hard, feeling a sense of accomplishment, and getting praised for doing well.

Sean: Yes, absolutely. I like to work hard and to have things to show for it.

Intern: I also wanted to point out that from what you have shared with me, what has also helped you is a strong inner voice that keeps pushing. Twice now you've told me about how, when faced with a challenge, you tell yourself to not give up and to keep going. That's an important motivator for you.

Sean: Hmm . . . I never thought of that. You are right. I do often remind myself to keep pushing ahead.

When people talk about abstract feeling states, such as self-hatred, exception finding centers on an actual event in which the client feels better. Therefore, the abstract state is translated into concrete behaviors that the client does, and the client can see that he is able to feel good about himself at times.

Example 5: The client's mother died six months ago, leaving him to be the sole caregiver for his father.

The client, Geoffrey, gets overwhelmed trying to run errands or complete paperwork for his father and then goes to sleep because he feels so stressed out.

Geoffrey: It feels like I'm having a nervous breakdown every day.

Intern: When are times that you feel a little better?

Geoffrey: When I'm at work. I have one project now, and I set my own hours, but I have deadlines for when things have to be completed.

Intern: You're making a lot of important points here. (She counts on her fingers.) So, you feel better when 1) you have one project going at a time, 2) you set some structure around the amount the time you work, and 3) when you have deadlines for when tasks need to be completed. Let's break those down. It sounds like it's easier for you when you do one project at a time. Right now, are you working on one part of your father's estate or a lot of different parts?

Geoffrey: A lot of different things—it makes my head scrambled, and I try to run around, but then I don't end up getting anything done.

Intern: So what's a priority to get done for your father right now? Maybe you can just focus on one thing at a time.

Geoffrey: I'd have to think about that, but it sounds like a good idea.

Intern: The second thing you mentioned is that you set your own hours. How could you apply that to taking care of your father's business?

Geoffrey: I guess that means I can't do it all day long. I can just take a portion of time each day and work on it.

Intern: Do you have some ideas about a time frame that sounds reasonable?

Geoffrey: Maybe an hour a day? I don't know if that will get everything done, though.

Intern: So an hour a day seems reasonable. How does that compare to how much time you're spending on it now?

Geoffrey: (Smiles ruefully) If I think about it, I'm not spending much time actually working on my dad's stuff. I spend more time worrying about it until I finally go to sleep to escape all the worry.

Intern: So an hour a day might even represent an improvement for you. Having deadlines was the third point you mentioned about what is helpful at work. What ideas do you have about how that might work with your dad's stuff?

Geoffrey: Some of it does have deadlines; that's what makes me such a nervous wreck.

Intern: I wonder how you can make that work for you, like at your job?

Geoffrey: I guess it's obvious, although I didn't see it before. I need to figure out what stuff has deadlines and then tackle those first.

Intern: You've come up with a lot of ideas that will hopefully make this seem easier. Just to make sure we're clear, can you summarize how you could take what works for you at your job and apply it to taking care of your father's affairs?

Geoffrey: Well, first I need to figure out what are the priorities, when I have to get certain things done.

Intern: How could you do that?

Geoffrey: I could make a list of all that needs doing, and the stuff with deadlines I could put into a calendar. Once I figure out what I need to do first, I'll just decide to work on that one thing rather than dwelling on everything else that needs to be done.

Intern: And what else?

Geoffrey: Set my own hours, like I do at work. I can decide that I'm going to spend an hour every day on it. At least I'll get something done rather than running around like a chicken with my head cut off or getting nothing done because it's all too much, and I end up falling asleep to forget about everything! I can even do a lot of this stuff at the office. I end up staying late anyway, so I'm not taking anything away from my job.

Intern: How would that be helpful to work on it at your job?

Geoffrey: Well, I'm already in "work" mode. I'm in my professional mode. If I approach it like work, I can make those phone calls and fill out some of the paperwork, just like I do at my job. Plus, I can't fall asleep!

Intern: You've come up with a lot of great ideas for how you can tackle your father's estate.

Example 6: Karla is a 25-year-old from El Salvador who was referred to the social work intern at a health clinic because of her doctor's concern about domestic violence. Karla revealed to the intern that she did not live with the father of her one-month-old baby, but that he helped her financially. Karla said she had no family in the United States or any other source of support other than her boyfriend's family. Karla mentioned that she had moved in with her boyfriend once before, but her boyfriend's constant use of marijuana and her nagging mother-in-law made her change her mind. Although her boyfriend was mad, she moved back to her apartment anyway. She confessed to the intern that her greatest fear is that her boyfriend will follow through on his threats to take custody of their child if Karla doesn't live with him.

Intern: Karla, has your boyfriend tried to take your child away from you in the past?

Karla: Yes, after I left him the first time I tried to live with him.

Intern: What happened?

Karla: He got really mad that I didn't want to stay with him, so he tried to come to my apartment to take the baby away. But I didn't let him.

Intern: What did you do to stop him from taking your child?

Karla: I talked to him. I told him that he wasn't going to be able to take care of the baby. I told him that it was a lot of work. I listed all the responsibilities there are in taking care of a child—the holding, rocking, feeding, changing diapers, going to the store, not getting sleep. Then, another time, he said he would go to court and get her taken away from me. I talked to him about his drug addiction. I said, "If you take me to court, I will tell the judge how often you smoke marijuana."

Intern: It sounds like you were successful in talking him out of taking away your child. How were you able to do that?

Karla: Because my baby comes first. I love her so much. I love my boyfriend too, but not as much as my baby.

This example shows that the intern was able to help Karla see that she had already successfully managed the situation she feared. The exception finding gave Karla concrete evidence that she had the strength and motivation to solve her problem.

All of these examples illustrate how finding exceptions—identifying times when the problem does not occur or times when things are a little better—can help the client generate a number of ideas about how to solve the problem, drawing from past experiences or strengths that have been used to solve other problems. Exception finding is a critical skill for a practitioner who recognizes the value of a strengths-based approach.

EXERCISES

Exercise 1: Mila is a young Latina who is involved in the child protective services (CPS) system for not going to doctors' appointments for her six-month-old child (medical neglect). In this brief scenario, how could you use exception finding?

> **Intern:** How was Kimberly's doctor appointment on Friday?
> **Mila:** It went well; they said her enzyme levels are stable, and I have another appointment on Friday.
> **Intern:** Oh good. How are you getting to your appointment this week?
> **Mila:** I called Medicaid and they are going to provide the transportation for my appointments from now on.
> **Intern:** Oh good. I'm glad you got that worked out.

Exercise 2: How could exception finding be used in the following intake that was conducted with an 18-year-old woman who left college due to feelings of depression?

> **Intern:** So what's going on?
> **Laura:** Well, I just left college because I was feeling really depressed and was having suicidal thoughts.
> **Intern:** How long has this been going on?
> **Laura:** It started when I got to school and had to go to the hospital down there a few weeks ago.

Intern: What hospital were you going to and how long did you stay?

Laura: I was going to [_____]. I was there for three days.

Intern: Oh okay. Are you currently having suicidal thoughts?

Laura: No.

Intern: How severe were these thoughts? Did you have a plan or ever attempt suicide?

Laura: No, I never attempted or had a plan. I was just feeling like I didn't care.

Intern: So you were feeling hopeless?

Laura: Yeah.

Intern: Can you tell me about your symptoms?

Laura: I've just been really down and depressed. I haven't been able to do much.

Intern: Have you been able to sleep?

Laura: Yeah.

Intern: What about your appetite? How has that been?

Laura: I haven't been able to eat much.

Intern: Have you lost or gained any weight?

Laura: Yeah, I've lost about 15 pounds since I was in the hospital.

Intern: Oh, wow. That's a lot. Do you have any substance-abuse issues?

Laura: No.

Intern: Do you have any family history of mental illnesses?

Laura: No.

CONCLUSION

In order to successfully help clients, we must fully understand them. We need to know about their problems, certainly, but we must also know what they bring to the work that will aid them in finding answers. Again, it is not our job to use our knowledge, experience, and strengths to solve client problems; it is our job to work with clients in a way that allows them to recognize their own resources and abilities to solve problems and improve their situations. Two techniques were discussed in this chapter that will help you elicit client strengths: a biopsychosocial-spiritual assessment with a strengths-based slant and exception-finding. Both of these are excellent methods of obtaining information about what is useful in clients' makeup, experiences, and situation that will uncover ideas about how to solve the problems that afflict them. It allows us and them to see not what is "wrong," but what is "right." Properly assessing a client's strengths is just as important as determining the client's problem.

PART 4

GOAL SETTING AND INTERVENTION

CHAPTER 7

GOAL SETTING

From the beginning of the book in Chapter 1 the importance of having a purpose for your work with clients was discussed. Additionally, the engagement phase of the helping process emphasizes an orientation toward the accomplishment of client goals (Chapter 2). This chapter continues the focus on goal setting with clients.

At the foundation level of social work practice, practitioners are often involved with assessing a client's needs for services so that appropriate referrals can be made, or in determining a client's eligibility for services. But, when you work with clients over time, there should be an orientation toward goals that goes beyond providing support and having a relationship with clients. Although the latter are important requirements for all ongoing client work, we also must help clients to change in some positive, meaningful way. The development of goals is critical for the following reasons (Hepworth et al., 2010):

- to provide focus to the work
- to get helper and client agreement about what should be done
- to monitor progress of the intervention
- to know when the work is complete

Exhibit 7.1 spells out some guidelines for goals.

EXHIBIT 7.1: **Guidelines for Goals**

---

1. Provide a rationale to client for why goals are needed.
2. The goal should be based upon a change in the client's behavior rather than what another person will do.
3. The goal should be one the client is motivated to pursue.
4. Choose only a couple of goals to start, prioritizing with the client's input.
5. Break large goals into several smaller goals. For example, the goal of leaving a violent relationship might entail obtaining job skills, finding employment, getting reliable transportation, and setting up child care.
6. State goals in terms of the presence of positive behaviors (following directions at school) rather than the absence of negative behaviors (stop acting out). This makes it clear what the client is to do and focuses away from the negative behavior.

7. Consider goals in terms of final outcome (using positive discipline methods) rather than the formal services in which clients will participate (attending a parenting group) (Christensen et al., 1999).
8. Match goals to client readiness.

   Although these guidelines all have importance, the next section will elaborate further on matching goals to client readiness.

MULTIPLE-CHOICE QUESTION

In relation to goals, what are some concerns with the child welfare scenario presented on pps 43–44?

A. A purpose has not been laid out for the contact.
B. The goals for custody (and after custody) are not made explicit.
C. Progress is not tied to the actions of the client but to a length of time.
D. The worker has not aligned herself with the client to achieve goals.
E. There may be duplication of services in working toward goals.
F. All of the above

MATCHING GOALS TO CLIENT READINESS

Chapter 5 on the decisional balance discussed choosing goals that match clients' readiness for change. If a person has not yet decided to change a behavior (e.g., seeking abstinence from substance use), then more immediate goals can be chosen (e.g., decreasing substance use; improving the client's non-using social network; bolstering alternative, healthy coping mechanisms). Additionally, if clients are unmotivated for change, goals may be oriented toward meeting the requirements of the mandate: "Whose idea was it that you come here? What does [_____] need to see in order to say that you don't have to come here anymore?"

The following example shows the need for people to be sensitive to a client's readiness to change.

Intern: I brought a bunch of stuff with me today that I hope will help you decide what you would like your next step to be. I know that you stated that you would like to remain in this county, so I've only brought information about treatment programs here.
Kim: I still just don't know about this. I'm not sure what I want to do yet.

Intern: What I understand from the last few times we've spoken is that you want to change your life, and you recognize that you have a problem. But you're still nervous about making that change by going into treatment. Is that pretty close to what you're feeling?

Kim: (Arms crossed) Yeah, basically.

Intern: You seem very put off by this whole conversation. I really don't expect you to make a decision today. It's something I know you need to think about. But I do want you to know what your options are.

Kim nods agreement.

Intern: I don't want you to feel overwhelmed; we're just going to go through the types of programs in the county. You don't have to make a decision today.

Kim: Okay.

Intern: There is the substance-abuse program at the health department that meets twice a week. These classes educate about addiction and are meant to help you build a support network of fellow recovering addicts and professionals, similar to Narcotics Anonymous meetings. If you decide to go this route, we just need to call to set up an assessment interview. There is also an inpatient program in the county that is 28 days long. This program does accept your medical assistance, so you wouldn't be responsible for paying. Again, if you chose this route we just need to set up an interview. This sound okay so far?

Kim: I know I need to do something. I just don't think I'm ready to do inpatient.

Intern: I know you had mentioned that you were in an inpatient facility in the past. Can you tell me about how that was for you?

Kim: I mean, it helped. I stayed clean for a while.

Intern: So it was helpful for you. What do you think might help you make the decision to give it a try again?

Kim: I don't know. I need to talk with my husband first.

Intern: That's fine. I think that it's important for you to keep all of your supportive family involved in this. And I want you to know that it's okay to be unsure. You have made a huge step in considering treatment and have come a long way in recognizing that this is a problem. How about we meet again on Friday, and by then you can let me know how the conversation went with your husband and we can go from there?

Kim: Thanks. Sorry I'm just not in a great mood today.

What do you conclude from this interaction about the client's readiness to enter a treatment program? The client indicates by her body language (crossing her arms in front of her) and her statements ("I still just don't know about this. I'm not sure what I want to do yet") that she is not ready to examine treatment options. Although the intern picked up on this and reflected her impressions, she did not stop going through the material she had collected. After successfully reflecting the client's feelings of reluctance, the social work intern could offer to explore with the client her ambivalence about change (see Chapters 4 and 5).

FUTURE-ORIENTED QUESTIONING

In order to set the frame for goal setting, a technique from solution-focused therapy, called future-oriented questions, can be posed. Future-oriented questions help clients develop a vision of a problem-free future. Seeing past the problem into the future assists clients in viewing alternative possibilities, which in turn gives them hope and helps them develop a blueprint for how to get there. In Exhibit 7.2, variations of future-oriented change questions are listed, and several examples of their implementation follow.

EXHIBIT 7.2: **Future-Oriented Change Questions**

Miracle Question	"If a miracle happened in the night while you were sleeping, but you didn't know this miracle had occurred, what would be the first thing you noticed when you woke up in the morning to let you know a miracle had occurred?" (de Shazer, 1998)
Dream Question	"Suppose that tonight while you are sleeping you have a dream. In this dream you discover the answers and resources you need to solve the problem that you are concerned about right now. When you wake up tomorrow, you may or may not remember your dream, but you notice you are different. As you go about starting your day, how will you know that you discovered or developed the skills and resources necessary to solve your problem? What will be the first small bit of evidence that you did this? Who will be the first person to notice that you have, and are using, some of the resources you discovered in your dream? What will they be noticing about you that will be evidence to them that you have, and are using, these resources?" (Greene et al., 1998, p. 397)
Variations of Future-Oriented, Hypothetical Questions	"Imagine yourself in the future when the problem is no longer a problem. Tell me where you are, what you are doing and saying, and what others around you are doing and saying."

The examples below illustrate the use of the different types of future-oriented questions. Note how, in each example, the questions help to change the way the client is initially feeling about his or her problem. Observe how goals arise from how the clients answer the questions.

Example 1: Marilyn is a single, Caucasian woman in her 50s who has a diagnosis of bipolar disorder.

Intern: So Marilyn, I know that right now is a really tough time. But when you're past this, and your life has changed to what you want, where do you see yourself? What do you see yourself doing?

Marilyn: Well, I really see myself working in a printing job like the one I had when I did that temp position. Boy! That was really a neat job. In printing there is a need for people who can do the public relations, and also know the printing part of it. I used to hate working with people, but my current job has really forced me to work with people, and now I like it. Also, I would really like to work with people dealing with loss and grief. Not everyone can deal with grief, but I can.

Intern: So you will have a different job?

Marilyn: Yes. And I have also wanted for some time to get involved with some volunteer work. I'm thinking I'd like to do some work with hospice. I can do that.

Intern: What else? Where do you see yourself?

Marilyn: Well, I'm going to have to sell the house. I guess I see myself in a smaller place, you know, like a one-bedroom apartment. I think that will be more manageable for me.

Intern: And looking back, what will you say you did to get beyond the difficulties?

Marilyn: I just keep plugging away. You've got to; there's no other choice but to do it.

The use of the future-oriented hypothetical question in the example with Marilyn illustrates how removing the constraints of the problem allows her to see the steps she can take to change her situation. It also gives her confidence, as you can see in the use of her decisive language ("I'm going to have to…").

Example 2: Kim is a 37-year-old Caucasian female who entered a county detox center to withdraw from alcohol and cocaine. She has a 14-year-old son who is currently in the custody of her ex-husband. Kim has a job waiting for her after she completes the 90-day treatment program she will be entering following detox.

Intern: Imagine you woke up tomorrow morning and while you had been sleeping a miracle happened and your problem was suddenly solved. The problem is gone, but because you were sleeping when this miracle happened, you don't know that it occurred. But you wake up tomorrow and you will be different. How will you know a miracle has happened?

Kim: I'd be sober and not hung over. I'd be in my own apartment, with my son.

Intern: What would your being sober look like?

> **Kim:** There wouldn't be any drugs or alcohol in the apartment, and I wouldn't be trying to figure how, when, or where I could get some. I wouldn't be thinking about them all the time.
>
> **Intern:** What would your apartment look like?
>
> **Kim:** It would be neat, picked up. I'd have prints on the wall.
>
> **Intern:** What would you do with your time instead of searching for drugs and alcohol?
>
> **Kim:** I'd spend it with my son. We could go shopping or I could watch him play basketball. I'd enjoy just being around him and talking.
>
> **Intern:** What would you talk to him about?
>
> **Kim:** I'd tell him I was sorry for messing up my life and his, but mainly I'd talk about whatever he wanted to talk about.
>
> **Intern:** What steps need to happen for even a small part of this miracle to happen?
>
> **Kim:** I'd have to complete treatment and make sure that I go to meetings to stay sober. I'd have to get a better job than I have now so that I can earn more money to support the two of us and find an apartment. I'd also have to go to court to show my ex that I'm responsible.

In the preceding example with the miracle question, the intern asks Kim to describe specific behaviors she would be doing to develop a picture of her life without the problem. This picture clearly lays the foundation for what Kim needs to accomplish and builds her motivation to take these steps.

> **Example 3:** Karla is a 25-year-old from El Salvador who was referred to the social work intern at a health clinic because of the doctor's concern about domestic violence. Karla revealed that she did not live with the father of her one-month-old baby, but that he helped her financially. Karla said she had no family in the United States or any other source of support other than her boyfriend's family. She confessed to the intern that her greatest fear was that her boyfriend would follow through on his threats that if Karla did not live with him, he would take custody of the child. The intern used the miracle question to help develop a picture of life without this problem, which in turn yielded a goal.
>
> **Intern:** We are going to do something different right now. I'm going to ask you to use your imagination. Is that okay?
>
> **Karla:** Sure.
>
> **Intern:** I want you to imagine that you are at home right now, and that your baby is asleep. You are very tired, so you go to sleep as well. Then, in the middle of the night, a miracle happens. Your problem is gone. It has disappeared completely. When you wake up in the morning, you don't know that a miracle has happened because you were sleeping. What is the first sign that tells you that a miracle has happened and that the problem is gone?

Karla: I guess I won't be scared that my boyfriend would take my child away from me.

Intern: What would be the first sign that tells you that your partner won't be taking your child away from you?

Karla: I'll have a court document that says I have custody of my child.

Intern: How did it happen that you got custody of your child?

Karla: The judge found out that my boyfriend constantly uses marijuana and that I was a better parent that he could ever be.

Intern: How did the judge find out about that?

Karla: Because my lawyer told him.

Intern: What would it take for you to start moving toward getting sole custody of your child?

Karla: I guess I need to talk to a lawyer about what is happening.

The use of the miracle question allows Karla to view herself in a different way. It allows her to recognize her strength as a mother and to feel positively about the possibility of having custody of her child. She is able to see beyond her fear and outline a strategy for taking action.

Example 4: Sean, age 18, was homeless after revealing his sexual orientation to his family. The intern helping Sean was placed at a homeless drop-in shelter.

Intern: Sean, I'm going to ask you a different kind of question, so bear with me for a few moments. Suppose that tonight you went to sleep and dreamt that you found the answers and the tools that you need to solve the problems you came here with. When you wake up, you feel that something has changed and you are different. As you start your day, how will you know that you have found the answers and the tools that you need to solve your problem? What will be the first thing that would tell you that something was different? Who will be the first person to notice that you are using some of the answers and tools that you found in your dream. What would they notice?

Sean: Well, in the morning I wake up and feel good about myself. I mean, really good. I feel confident that I am a good person and I'm confident in my abilities.

Intern: And what will you be doing when you wake up feeling so good and confident about yourself?

Sean: Hmmm... I don't know.

Intern: Let's say I am watching you through a video camera, what will I see you doing or saying to yourself?

Sean: I will be so happy that I will tell myself that I have a new start on life. I will tell myself that I'm a good person. I will believe it and know it in my heart to be true.

Intern: And what do you do next?

Sean: I continue throughout my day feeling confident and happy about myself as I do chores around the house and go to work.

Intern: What will it look like when you are confident and happy as you go about doing these things?

Sean: Normally, I would be reluctant to do any chores, and I would procrastinate, but this day I will do them without being reluctant. I see a smile on my face and a spring in my step. I even see myself chuckling and listening to my favorite music. When I go to work, I am still smiling and I can't wait to tell people how good I feel. I will share it with all my work friends, and I would even call my close friends to let them know the good news.

Intern: And who will be the first to notice the change?

Sean: Well, if I had to work that day my boss and fellow waiters will see a change. They will see me as more confident in my abilities and more talkative. If I were with my friends instead of at work, they will see that I carry myself more confidently and talk about myself more highly.

Intern: So, you would be more talkative with others. Who specifically would you be talking to?

Sean: While at work I talk with all of my coworkers. Although I do really well at work, I don't chit-chat a lot with others. But today I feel confident and happy, so I talk to all of the other waiters on duty. There are two guys there that I have become work friends with, so I will talk more with them. Also, there is another guy there that I have always wanted to be friends with, perhaps more, but have shied away from talking to him, but this day I feel confident and I go talk to him.

Intern: What would you say to your friends and to this new guy?

Sean: I tell my friends how good I feel. And they can see it. They can see that I am happier. That guy that I've been wanting to talk to, I go over to him and start up a basic conversation. I smile, see if he's interested, and maybe we can go out for a bite to eat after work.

Intern: So, it seems to me that your confidence and happiness will help you become more sociable and even open things up for a possible romance.

Sean: Yes, I see myself doing that. Going out on a limb and taking a chance. I have the courage that day.

Intern: You mentioned being with your close friends. What will they say?

Sean: They notice that I am happier and confident, and that makes them happy. They encourage me to keep doing whatever it is I was doing to make me happy about me.

Intern: And when you say they would see you as more confident and happy, what would that look like?

Sean: They would see me smiling and joking with them. They would hear me laughing and playing around like old times.

Intern: What would you be saying when hanging out with them?

Sean: I tell them of my newfound confidence. I tell them that I have a new perspective on life and a new chance. That things around me look brighter and better than they have in years. And they would tell me that they were worried about me for a long time, because I was so unhappy with myself and they knew it. And now they are glad that I am happy and have a positive outlook on life.

Intern: Then what will you do?

Sean: At the end of the day I come home and still feel good about myself and fall asleep feeling confident and hopeful that tomorrow will be the same.

Intern: What will you be doing or saying to yourself during this time?

Sean: I come home smiling. I tidy up around the house, which I am usually reluctant to do, and I get on the Internet and chat with some friends online. When I go to sleep, I tell myself that I have had a wonderful day. I tell myself that tomorrow will be another great day, and I know that it is true. And rather than any negative thoughts about myself at night, I can sleep knowing in my heart that I am a good person who has a lot to offer.

Intern: Sean, that sounds like a wonderful sequence. I wonder, when are times/ instances that you can think of where a little piece of this dream has come true already?

Note in this example how, when Sean seemed stuck and unable to describe what he would be doing if the problem were removed, the intern used the "video camera" question. ("Let's say I am watching you through a video camera, what will I see you doing or saying to yourself?") This can be a useful way of helping the client describe specific behaviors, as well as the feelings that accompany them. The intern also explored the contextual details of the miracle, with the recognition that we are part of social systems and our actions influence— and are influenced by—those around us.

In all four examples, the interns used future-oriented questions. In each one, the intern asks the client to paint a picture of what his or her life looks like without the problem, and the client is able to see the positive effect this has. By "removing the problem," the client is, in effect, seeing his or her life in a different way, past the problem, into solutions.

EXERCISE FOR YOUR PRACTICE

Which of the three future-oriented types of questions would you be comfortable using with a client? Why have you chosen this particular one?

SCALING QUESTIONS

Scaling questions encapsulate a number of techniques and are a powerful tool for goal setting and quantifying progress. When people are besieged by problems, they feel overwhelmed. Scaling questions reduce problems to manageable proportions due to the measureable and concrete nature of the scale. Scaling questions involve the following:

- choosing a goal
- constructing a scale around a goal
- anchoring the goal
- rank ordering and exception finding
- relationship questions and discussing any discrepancies
- task setting
- measurement

An example, applying the scenario with Sean, the 18-year-old gay man who was homeless after his parents rejected his "coming out," will illustrate the use and effectiveness of scaling questions.

Construct a scale around a goal: Verbally and in writing describe a 1-to-10 scale around a goal you have developed with the client. Phrase the goal in terms of the presence of a positive, but one that is not in superlative terms. For example, if a person is depressed, talking about "feeling full of joy" might be seen as too extreme and unrealistic.

Example:

> **Intern:** Sean, let's say this scale from 1 to 10 represents your goal of "feeling better about yourself."

Anchor the goal: Anchor "10" as "when the goal will be achieved" or "when the problem is no longer a problem." A focus on "10" allows clients who previously viewed their problems as "hopeless" and "overwhelming" to concretely see the possibility of change, which gives them hope for the future. To operationalize the goal, ask clients to describe in concrete and specific terms three behaviors and thoughts they will be having when they have reached "10." The reason behaviors and thoughts are a focus is that they are seen as more under clients' control than are feelings. When we ask clients to describe behaviors and thoughts, for the most part, we want them to identify the presence of positive behaviors rather than the absence of negative behaviors.

Example:

> **Intern:** What will you be doing? What does 10 look like for you?
> **Sean:** I will feel good about who I am on a consistent basis. I will think more positive thoughts about myself. I will accept that fact that I am gay.
> **Intern:** Let's beak this down a bit. What three things would you be doing to show that you feel good about yourself, that you are thinking more positively, and that you accept your sexual orientation?
> **Sean:** That's a tough one.

> **Intern:** Think about what you would be doing differently or saying differently to yourself.
>
> **Sean:** I would be more friendly and outgoing, so I would hang out with friends more often. And not just the friends that I have, but I would make new friends. I would also start dating again. I have felt so badly about myself that I haven't dated or even felt confident enough to ask a guy out, so I would start dating. And then, finally, I would be taking better care of my body, such as eating healthier and exercising at least three times a week.
>
> **Intern:** So to recap, you would be more sociable and make new friends, you would start dating again, and you would take better care of your body through diet and exercise.

Note that the intern helped Sean focus on positive things he will be doing rather than negative things he will no longer be doing.

Rank ordering and exception finding: Clients then rank themselves in relation to "10." Clients will often place themselves at a number that would imply that change has already occurred, and this can be used to help them see that their problems are not as all-encompassing as previously believed. You can inquire about the resources people have employed to get to where they are with questions such as "So you're already a 4? What have you been doing to get yourself there?" Occasionally, clients place themselves at a "1"; in these cases, the practitioner can ask what the person is doing to prevent problems from getting even worse. Of note is that you do not challenge people on their ratings. For instance, you would not say, "A 7? You are not!" The way to get at discrepancy is to ask relationship questions, which are covered in the next section.

Example:

> **Intern:** So, tell me where you currently place yourself on that scale?
>
> **Sean:** I'd say a 4. Again, some days I might place myself higher or lower.
>
> **Intern:** That's okay, Sean. It's one step at a time. There are good days and then there can be not-so-good days. Being a 4 on this scale, how have you managed to get that high?
>
> **Sean:** Well, accomplishing things at work helps, being around my friends, and also knowing that I have made it so far without my family. How many 18-year-olds do you know who can rise above homelessness, find a job and a place to live, and be okay?
>
> **Intern:** You are very resourceful and highly motivated. Those are significant strengths you possess. And from the way it sounds, those strengths are what have you at a 4 today!
>
> **Sean:** Definitely.

Relationship questions involve asking people to rate themselves on their scale from the viewpoint of another person that is invested in their change. Very often, clients view themselves differently from how others experience them. Getting clients to perceive themselves from someone else's perspective may help them see themselves more realistically.

Task setting calls upon clients to determine how they will move up one rank order by the time of the next contact.

Example:

Intern: So, how will move you from a 4 to a 5 by our next session?

Sean: Keep thinking positive. Keep pushing myself ahead, believing that I'm going to be all right. And remind myself when I start to feel badly about myself how far I have come in the last year.

Intern: And what will that look like, Sean? What will you be doing at a 5 that's different from your 4?

Sean: I guess by thinking positively I will feel a bit better about myself, which will help me get out of the house. I will be slightly more sociable and call my friends to get together.

Intern: Ok, so your 5 is that positive thinking will motivate you to be more sociable with your friends.

Sean: Yes.

Intern: I think that sounds wonderful. And you brought up a technique that many use without knowing it, called positive self-talk. It's telling yourself positive messages such as, "look how far I've come in the past year." That kind of thinking can be very helpful for many. So, try these things you have mentioned over the course of the week and be mindful of how you are thinking and feeling about yourself. Next week we'll meet again and check in on the same scale to see where you are at and where you'd like to go.

Measurement of progress: The scale should be preserved in the case file with a copy given to the client. At each contact, the practitioner can check in with clients regarding where they are on their scale and on their completion of tasks. Progress continues to be monitored, which makes attainment of goals quantifiable and measurable. Some of the potential pitfalls associated with using scaling interventions are listed in Exhibit 7.3.

EXHIBIT 7.3: **Scaling Questions: Pitfalls and Solutions**

Deciding which goal is a priority for the client (working on the client's anger management)	Allow the client to determine the priority goal (working on managing the children's behavior).
Phrasing the goal in terms of absence of negatives ("when the client is not feeling depressed")	Phrase the goal in terms of presence of positives ("feeling better").
Not fleshing out a detailed picture of "10" (when the problem the client came for is solved)	Find at least three behavioral indicators of what will be happening when the problem is solved; use videotape analogy so that clients can visualize positives ("If I was looking through a video player, what would I see you doing?").
Talking about when everything is "perfect"	Concentrate on "when the problem the client came for is solved."
Anchoring each point in the 10-point continuum	Simply spend time anchoring "10" to get clients focused on where they are heading.

Wanting to convince the client of a different rank ordering that is perceived as unrealistic (either too high or low)	Take client's rank ordering at face value; use relationship questions to get at disparities (for example, a child might rank themselves at 7, but rank a parent's perception at 3); then focus on what is needed to move one number up on the scale.
Not using the full range of techniques within the scaling question	Use anchoring, rank ordering, relationship questions, exception finding, complimenting, and task setting.
Failing to track the scale over time	Measure the client's progress by tracking numbers on the scale over time.
Not taking advantage of the many uses to which scaling questions can be put	Scale goals, confidence, motivation.

EXERCISE FOR YOUR PRACTICE

Consider a client goal and work through the steps of the solution-focused scale hypothetically.

1. Choose a goal:
2. Construct a 1–10 point scale:
3. Anchor 10 with three concrete behaviors:
4. Rank order:
5. Discuss exceptions:
6. Use relationship questions and discuss any discrepancies:
7. Set a task that would represent a one-point movement on the scale:

CONCLUSION

This chapter discussed goal setting with clients, which is an important part of the helping process, particularly when the work with clients is ongoing over time. Assisting clients in developing goals is critical so that our work with them proceeds in a positive and meaningful direction. Solution-focused interventions—namely future-oriented questions and scaling questions—have been detailed here because of the ways that they can assist people in constructing a vision of how they would like their lives to change as a result of the work we do together.

CHAPTER 8

INTERVENTION: PROBLEM SOLVING

The next few chapters get into the heart of your work with clients—the intervention phase. A theme of this work is to collaborate with clients so that you only facilitate their change rather than decide what is best for people and apply your expert knowledge accordingly. Instead, you want to solicit people's ideas about how to improve their situations and allow them to take responsibility for the ideas and the change efforts. Your role is to help them develop a change plan and to apply it—the topic of the intervention chapters.

PROBLEM SOLVING

As much as possible, you should seek clients' input into ideas about how they can solve a problem or get around an obstacle. One of social work's values is that we must work to cultivate self-determination; to the degree possible, clients should be the ones to come up with the solutions that fit their needs, circumstances, and strengths. Further, our job is to help people find ways to help themselves. If they can successfully develop problem-solving skills, you will help them not only with their immediate problem, but also with future problems that inevitably will arise.

The introduction of this book laid out that the problem-solving process (Perlman, 1957) is an underlying framework for *Helping Skills for Social Work Direct Practice*. To make a distinction, the problem-solving process that will be referred to in this chapter is a technique from behavioral theory that is often used as a standalone intervention or as part of a package of cognitive-behavioral therapy (D'Zurilla & Nezu, 2001). In this context, problem-solving involves the process of defining the problem, brainstorming potential solutions to the problem, narrowing down the potential solutions to an agreed-upon option to implement and, finally, the implementation of the plan.

Problem solving can be done with individuals, families, or groups. Families often become stuck arguing about the same problems without finding solutions to them, so problem solving is ideal to use in these situations. In groups, members often have a tendency to give advice to each other ("This is what I would do in your situation" or "You should/need to do this"). Problem solving as a group around a particular individual's problem or, even better, around a problem that group members share, such as finding affordable housing, jobs, or dealing with transportation or child care barriers, can help members work around a particular barrier, while at the same time learning the problem-solving process, which they can then generalize to other situations.

DECIDING IF PROBLEM SOLVING IS RELEVANT

Problem solving is appropriate when there is a problem to be solved that is, at least to some degree, under the person's control. For instance, an intern in a child welfare setting worked with Sam, a boy in foster care, who was slated for adoption by his current foster parents. The intern decided to problem-solve about whether Sam's adoption by the foster parents was the right choice or not. This was a decision that had already been made and over which neither the intern nor Sam had control. A more helpful and appropriate intervention in this situation would have been to process his feelings about the adoption, what it meant for him, and to work on developing his communication skills so that he could discuss his feelings and concerns with his foster parents and other people involved in his care.

STEPS OF PROBLEM SOLVING

The steps involved in problem solving include:

1. defining the problem
2. brainstorming
3. evaluation of alternatives
4. selection of strategies
5. evaluation of selection

Exhibit 8.1 discusses some of the potential pitfalls to be avoided as you start using the problem-solving process with clients.

DEFINING THE PROBLEM

Once you have determined that problem solving is the appropriate technique, the next step is to define the problem. An important part of this step is to determine the "real problem," i.e., what is behind the problem or what caused it. An intern in a hospital setting identified

EXHIBIT 8.1: Problem-Solving: Pitfalls and Solutions

Pitfalls	Solutions
Taking on a superficial problem	Try to find the real problem (if being late to work is caused by children not being ready in the morning or having conflict with spouse in the morning, then the latter problems should be addressed).
Making the problem too vague and general (my teen daughter is impossible)	Take on one specific problem at a time, phrased in the positive (to get my teen daughter to do her chores); break complex problems into separate components.
During brainstorming, not coming up with enough solutions	Allow the client to come up with as many solutions as possible; mention that they can be silly, creative, outlandish, etc.; ask the client relationship questions (what would other people he/she knows say is a possible solution); have the practitioner make an off-the-wall solution to spur the creative process; if more than one person is taking part in the process, make sure to get feedback from everyone.
During brainstorming, people start criticizing ideas	Remind clients that this is the brainstorming phrase, and later they can evaluate their ideas; when people criticize, ask them to come up with an alternative solution instead.
An idea is selected, but not implemented.	Flesh out the details of the plan in writing, practice any skills necessary, determine barriers, and gain a commitment from the client.

(some ideas adapted from Foster & Robin (1998))

as a problem her client's 11-year-old son having a tantrum each evening when the client has a drink. The client's son is suffering from cancer, and the client, Georgia, is heavily involved in her son's care, which involves spending a lot of time with him each day, since his illness keeps him from going to school. Understandably, Georgia feels stressed and overwhelmed and, to manage these feelings, she has a couple of drinks in the evening to relax. Therefore, the "real problem" is that the client needs to find a way to manage her stress without drinking.

Another piece of defining the problem is to pick a manageable problem, or to partition the larger problem into smaller ones that can be tackled one at a time. For instance, if a person is trying to leave a violent relationship, she may also need help in finding reliable child care and transportation, as well as housing and income. These could all be separate components targeted for problem solving.

A final piece of defining the problem is to select a problem that is of importance to the client, not necessarily what you believe to be the most critical problem. For instance, an intern placed at a faith-based organization that provided emergency services worked with Rita, a single, middle-aged, African American woman who needed assistance with food, her medical prescriptions, dental care, utility assistance, rental assistance, credit repair, and employment. However, her most pressing complaint was her arguments with her adult-age daughter, who was hanging around with people in trouble with the law, skipping her community college classes, and staying out all night. Rita said she was unable to concentrate on any of her other problems because of how upset she felt about her daughter. Therefore, the deteriorating relationship with her daughter became the problem to be solved.

BRAINSTORMING

The second step of problem solving is brainstorming, which involves generating and writing down all the possible solutions, regardless of their actual feasibility. The goal of this exercise is to get clients to come up with ideas by prompting them with statements, such as "Right now, we're just coming up with ideas, so you can just throw out anything, even if it seems ridiculous or impossible. We just want to come up with as long a list as possible." Other prompts to get the client to come up with more ideas are to ask relationship questions, such as "What would your mother/teacher/caseworker say you could do about this?" and about previous problem-solving attempts: "How did you solve a problem like this in the past?" You can also ask clients about what they think would *not* work: "What would you never do?" "What would never work?" The rationale is to get people to side with the resistance they have against coming up with ideas and change. As discussed in motivational interviewing (Miller & Rollnick, 2002), people will often speak out of the other side of their ambivalence—the part that wants to change—when you get them to talk about how change is not possible or desired.

Encourage spontaneity and creativity by cautioning people to avoid critical comments, such as "Yes, but . . ." and "That wouldn't work because . . ." Remind people that they will have a chance to look more closely at their ideas in the next step, but right now you want to generate as many solutions as possible. You can suggest possible solutions, as well, but make sure that the client is heavily involved in the process of coming up with ideas.

When working with a family or a group, the social worker should ask everyone in the room to give brainstorming ideas, perhaps proceeding in a "round-robin" fashion so that everyone's opinion is heard in turn. Rounds can be repeated as necessary until a sufficient number of ideas have been generated. For people in the room who are resistant or passive, ask them to assume roles that involve participation in the process, such as writing down alternatives.

As an example of brainstorming, the intern and Georgia, the client who has difficulty de-stressing without alcohol, came up with the following ideas:

1. hire a babysitter
2. exercise
3. play sports
4. sign up for a class
5. go on a cruise
6. take a vacation
7. go shopping
8. eat
9. spend time in nature
10. be around animals

11. garden
12. watch TV
13. have sex
14. spend time with a friend
15. go to dinner with an adult companion
16. talk on the phone to friends
17. call the intern
18. call a hotline
19. take a walk
20. take a bath
21. read
22. go to a movie
23. meditate
24. use relaxation techniques
25. find respite care

EVALUATION OF ALTERNATIVES

The next phase is to evaluate the alternatives. The first step here is to cross out patently irrelevant or impossible items. Georgia was overweight and already tended to use food as a coping mechanism, so the intern crossed out "eat." Georgia was also short on money, so "going on a cruise" and "taking a vacation" were not options currently. They explored many of the other ideas on the list, however.

SELECTION OF STRATEGIES

After discussion of the viable items, the next phase is to select one or more strategies that could help solve the problem. If more than one person is involved and the parties come to an impasse on a certain solution—one side wants one idea implemented and the other side wants another—ask the couple or the family members to implement one solution one week (usually the children's) and, if it doesn't work, to try the next idea the following week. Of note here is that you may not agree with the client on the best strategy to implement. For example, with Rita, the woman who complained about the relationship with her daughter, the intern preferred direct methods that involved mother and daughter learning better communication skills and resolving their differences. However, Rita chose the solution of "ignoring her daughter's behaviors and avoiding her daughter." She said that in order to maintain her health and to be able to focus on her other problems, she needed to keep calm, and avoiding arguments was the best way to do this.

To return to the example of Georgia de-stressing without alcohol, Georgia liked the idea of taking a walk around the neighborhood when she started to feel overwhelmed and frustrated. She was also amenable to signing up for a yoga class at her local recreational center and for the intern to teach her about other relaxation techniques. Georgia hadn't realized that she could reach out for support from the intern when she felt herself becoming overwhelmed. Since the intern wasn't available every day, the intern also provided her with the number to a crisis hotline. Georgia realized that having a tub bath was a lot more relaxing than her usual showers; she therefore decided to switch to taking a bath at night after her son went to bed rather than a hurried shower in the morning. The intern agreed to find available resources for respite care, and Georgia would ask local teenagers their interest in babysitting for a couple of hours weekly so she could go with her friends to dinner one night a week.

EVALUATION OF THE SELECTION

The next step of the problem-solving process is to evaluate the implemented option(s). The intern said she would check in at their following contact to see how Georgia had been able to de-stress using some of the ideas and tools they had come up with. She also planned that the next contact would involve talking about relaxation techniques and sharing with Georgia respite resources.

EXERCISE FOR YOUR PRACTICE

What client situation have you encountered that would be appropriate for problem solving and explain why?

OPEN-ENDED QUESTIONS FOR GENERATING IDEAS

Even if you decide not to follow the formal problem-solving process, you can still help people come up with their own ideas and answers through the use of open-ended questions. Considerable time was spent in Chapter 3 on the importance of being able to construct open-ended questions. Their usefulness is seen again when working with clients to problem-solve their challenges and obstacles. Open-ended questions are critically important in empowering clients to come up with choices that work for them.

The use of open-ended questions for uncovering potential solutions is demonstrated in the following group intervention with adults who are currently experiencing homelessness and living in a family shelter.

Group Leader 1: Welcome back, everyone. This week we will be discussing some of the barriers you may have experienced in obtaining employment, and we will brainstorm ways to overcome these barriers.

Group Leader 2: Who would like to begin?

Barbara: I'll start. Well, I tried to apply to a job at a department store, and I had to do the application on a computer at the store. I felt stupid because I am not very good at using a computer. I did not see the point of filling out the application online because I am not going to be using computers on the floor. I got really frustrated, so halfway through I just left.

Group Leader 1: Those computer applications can be really frustrating.

Annie: Yeah, I've had to use those computers before. They really suck.

Barbara: Did you get through it?

Annie: Yeah, but it took a really long time. I just breathed and took my time. Don't worry if it takes you 30 minutes or two hours; there is no time limit. I really needed this job, so I kind of didn't have a choice but to stick with it. I took an hour to fill out mine.

Group Leader 2: That sounds like a good way to handle the stress of filling out the job application.

Kelley: I'll go next. One time I showed up late for an interview because it was raining and the buses were running late. I was soaked to the bone, my makeup was running, and I looked like crap. I knew I wasn't going to get the job looking like this, so I just turned right around and got back on that bus. What's the point of sitting through an interview when I know I'm going to get rejected?

Emily: Yeah, I would have done the same thing. The darn buses can't stay on schedule even when it isn't raining. If you know they're not going to hire you, why waste your time?

Group Leader 1: So it sounds like the reliability of public transportation is a barrier. What are some ways to overcome this barrier?

Kelley: I don't know.

Emily: I guess maybe leaving earlier?

Group Leader 2: That's a good suggestion.

Kelley: Call and reschedule if I know I'm going to be late.

Emily: Or call, apologize, and let them know that you are running late.

Bryan: Whatever. That won't work. They don't care about people like us. There are thousands of people like us waiting to snatch up those jobs. We're totally replaceable.

Group Leader 1: What are the benefits of letting a potential employer know about the delay?

Annie: It shows respect.

Bryan: Why should I respect them if they don't respect me back? A couple months ago I was working at a drugstore. I was working really hard and was doing great on the job. Then we had a few days of bad weather and the buses kept being late. By the time I got to work I was two hours late. The first time they told me to call if that happens, so

I called the next time and they got mad! That's messed up. I did what they told me to do. It's not my fault if the buses can't get to the stops to pick me up. And I don't know anyone with a car, so I couldn't get a ride from someone. They fired me in the middle of my shift. I was finally there and working hard, but they didn't care. They fired me anyways. Jerks!

Group Leader 2: I'm sorry that happened. What barriers are you facing while trying to find employment?

Bryan: My wife and kids are nagging me to get a job. I might get kicked out of the shelter if I don't find one soon.

Group Leader 2: It sounds like you have motivation to find a job. What steps can you take to find employment?

Bryan: I went to the employment center at South County for help looking for jobs. They helped me find a job at a restaurant, but I didn't have the money to buy nice black slacks and the special non-slip shoes they require.

Barbara: I've had that problem before too, but actually I got set up with an appointment at Dress for Change, and they helped me find clothes.

Group Leader 1: That's a good suggestion. Can anyone else relate to this barrier?

The next example reinforces the technique of asking open-ended questions to help the client elicit potential ways of dealing with her problem situation.

Example: Mariana was a 29-year-old undocumented woman from El Salvador who was referred to a social worker by her OB/GYN doctor due to sad affect. Mariana was a first-time mom in her 30th week of pregnancy whose fetus was diagnosed with cleft palate. At the time of our first session, Mariana had lived in the U.S. with only her husband and a brother in the area. Mariana did not work. She and her husband lived in the living room of a two-bedroom apartment. Mariana's husband worked in construction, and his income barely paid for rent, food, and clothing.

Intern: Mariana, tell me what you would like to get out of talking to me today?

Mariana: I don't want to be worried about my child's problem.

Intern: How can you make that happen?

Mariana: I guess I can start looking for information about cleft palate. I want to understand the problem a little bit more.

Intern: That sounds great. How can you find more information on cleft palate?

Mariana: I can go back to the doctor and ask more questions. I can look on the Internet for more details. I guess those are things I could do.

Mariana went on to say that she became so emotional when the doctor said her child would be born with a problem that she couldn't hear the information he provided.

Intern: During your conversation with the doctor, was there a moment in which you felt less frustrated?

Mariana: I guess so. He said my child could have surgery and that gave me a little hope.

Intern: That sounds like a really important piece of information.

Mariana: Yes. I was really upset and that helped me feel better.

Intern: Good! Was there something else during your conversation that might have helped you feel better?

Mariana: I don't remember. I guess he said I could come back and ask more questions.
I was thinking about going to visit him again soon.

Intern: Good! Do you have a time frame for when you would like to do that?

Mariana: When I leave your office, I can make an appointment. I was also thinking I could make a list of questions that I might ask, just so I don't forget.

Intern: I think that is a great idea.

Mariana met with the doctor a few days after talking with the intern and saw the intern after that.

Intern: So you met with your doctor.

Mariana: Yes, I did. I tried hard not to cry when he was explaining what was happening to my child. I can't believe I didn't listen before.

Intern: You sound a lot better today. It sounds like the meeting was very productive.

Mariana: Yes, it was. He showed me some pictures of children with cleft palate. It was hard. But then he showed me some pictures of children after surgery, and they looked better. They have scars, but it's not too bad.

Intern: I'm glad things went well with your doctor. You seem calmer today.

Mariana: Yes, I am. I continue to feel sad, though. I still can't believe this is happening to us.

Intern: You're still feeling very sad about the prospect of your child being born with a cleft palate. And you're in shock about it too. Those are very normal reactions when first learning of this.

Mariana: There are lots of things I need to do to get ready.

Intern: What can you do?

Mariana: I think I could talk to the specialist that the doctor recommended to start arranging my child's surgery.

Intern: That sounds like a great idea.

Both of these examples illustrate how open-ended questions help clients come up with possible solutions that work for their individual situations. They allow clients to think of alternative ways of looking at their problems, thus empowering them to come up with ideas that fit their unique worldview.

EXERCISES

Exercise 1: This scenario takes place at a detoxification program for people who are dependent on alcohol and/or drugs. The intern is talking with Mark, who has gone through detox and is now facing treatment. How could she use open-ended questioning to get him to problem-solve?

Intern: How are you feeling about going to Pratt (the residential treatment program)?

Mark: Good. I'm looking forward to having less downtime. I hear it's more structured and that there is more to do than just sit around a watch a movie. I think they have a gym; that will be good, so I can work off my anxiety instead of eating when I'm anxious.

Intern: When do you feel anxious?

Mark: I'm just an anxious guy.

Intern: Are you feeling anxious about going to Pratt?

Mark: A little, since it's a new place, and I'm worried about defending myself.

Intern: What do you mean you're nervous about defending yourself?

Mark: I heard that you get thrown out of the program for defending yourself, even if you're not the person who initiated the fight.

Intern: So you are feeling anxious because you don't want to be thrown out of treatment for a fight you didn't start?

Mark: Yes. I don't want to get thrown out, but I don't want to be taken advantage of either.

Intern: You appear to be worried about this possibility; that's understandable. Nobody likes to get in trouble for something that wasn't their fault. What are some ideas you have to help you eliminate this fear?

Mark: I'm not sure . . . stay away from someone who doesn't like me.

Intern: I wonder if, in addition to staying away from someone, you could ask the staff for a suggestion of what you should do if someone is bothering you.

Mark: That's a good idea. I'll try and do that.

Exercise 2: Joan is a 41-year-old Caucasian female who has been diagnosed with paranoid schizophrenia. She is stabilized with medications and therapy, and currently resides at a transitional shelter for women. In this instance, the intern worked with Joan's fear of being in a busy train station en route to visiting her parents. As you read through the dialogue, think of ways to have the client come up with more ideas before the intern intercedes.

Intern: Now, let's do a what-if scenario and say, for example, that you arrive at Penn Station and you become confused. Try to brainstorm and think about all of the different things that you could do . . . and try to not judge what you are thinking; just let it flow.

Joan: I would freak out.

Intern: Okay. That's a possible outcome. What are some other things that you could do in that situation? Try to think of at least six things.

Joan: I could get back on a train and go home. I could . . . ask for help. I could get sick and throw up on the floor. I don't know what to do.

Intern: You are doing great.

Joan: I can't think of anything else.

Intern: May I make a few suggestions?

Joan: Sure.

Intern: You could stop, try to calm yourself by doing some deep breathing, and tell yourself that you are going to be okay.

Joan: What, like talk to myself?

Intern: Sure. You can use it when you are feeling overwhelmed. Many people do it all the time in different scenarios without even realizing it. It's really beneficial. You could say something like, "I'm going to get through this" or "I'll be fine." But back to some other options for you . . . you could look for signs. You could find security personnel to direct you. You could find a pay phone to call your dad's cell. You could . . .

Joan: (interrupting) Oh yeah! I forgot about my dad's cell phone! I'm sure there would have to be pay phones all around the station. I would be bound to find one. And maybe someone would let me use their cell if I couldn't find a pay phone. I could call my dad and he could come and find me.

Intern: That's a great solution! So, out of all the options that we talked about, which would you choose?

Joan: Well . . . I'd choose to stay calm and find a phone and call my dad.

Intern: That's wonderful. How confident are you that you can try that should you become confused?

Joan: I feel very confident that I can try that. That is an easy solution.

Intern: So should this occur, you are confident that you can try that option. That's great!

Joan: Yeah, I guess there are other things that I could do besides freak out.

Exercise 3: Seth is a six-year-old boy who has been living at his current foster care placement for one year. In the following scenario, how could you prompt the child for more ideas?

> **Intern:** How have you been doing at school?
> **Seth:** I pushed someone with my lunchbox. He was singing baby songs and it was annoying.
> **Intern:** What can you do instead of pushing him?
> **Seth:** Tell the teacher.
> **Intern:** What else can you do?
> **Seth:** I don't know.
> **Intern:** Remember what I told you at your day care? You can ignore the negative behavior. You did a really good job with that there.
> **Seth:** Yeah.

Exercise 4: Maharene is a 35-year-old Ethiopian female who came to the United States three years ago under the assumption of having a good job in place. However, she was trafficked, sold into domestic servitude, and kept as a slave for a year until she escaped. Shortly thereafter, she entered into an apartment transition program. Maharene struggles with the fear of running into the people who trafficked her. Therefore, she isolates herself in her apartment and will leave only to go to work, the grocery store, or the program for classes. Even though she is religious and very lonely, she will not participate in Ethiopian church services. In fact, she is particularly adverse to the Ethiopian community because her traffickers were Ethiopian.

In the following dialogue, change the social worker's questions to open-ended questions that help the client explore her own ideas and options.

> **Intern:** How have you been doing?
> **Maharene:** Good.
> **Intern:** You are now working full-time, which is wonderful. And you will soon be graduating from our program.
> **Maharene:** Yes, and I get compliments from the customers.
> **Intern:** That is great! Have you been doing anything to find an apartment?
> **Maharene:** Yes, but I have not found anything that I can afford.
> **Intern:** Maybe you should look for a basement apartment in a house.
> **Maharene:** No, that bothers my head.

> **Intern:** Why does it bother your head?
>
> **Maharene:** It is dark. No windows.
>
> **Intern:** You do not like basement apartments because they are dark and depressing.
>
> **Maharene:** Yes, yes, depressing.
>
> **Intern:** I see.
>
> **Maharene:** Sometimes I call places, but they cannot understand my English.
>
> **Intern:** Do you have a friend who can help you make phone calls while looking for an apartment?
>
> **Maharene:** Yes, but she is always working when I am off.
>
> **Intern:** Do you have anyone else that might be able to help you make phone calls and set up appointments?
>
> **Maharene:** (bursts into tears) No, I do not have anybody here. My family is all in Ethiopia.
>
> **Intern:** Let's sit down.
>
> **Maharene:** I am sorry.
>
> **Intern:** It is okay. Anyone in your situation would feel this way. I know you are Christian. Do you belong to a church here?
>
> **Maharene:** No, I cannot understand them.
>
> **Intern:** A church might be a good way for you to meet some good people, even if you do not understand every word they say.

The inclusion of open-ended questions in this dialogue would allow the client more opportunity to figure out how she might go about solving the problems that afflict her—most importantly finding an affordable apartment. It is difficult to predict how the changes made here would affect the client, but it could be that the succession of closed-ended questions resulted in the client feeling more hopeless about her ability to solve the problem. Instead, opening up the possibilities might have acted to free up the client's problem-solving capacities rather than shutting them down.

CONCLUSION

Problem solving—either using the formal process or simply being sure to ask open-ended questions to get clients to think for themselves—turns out to be a critical piece of intervention. If we, as social workers, are successful, our results in this area are twofold: we help clients solve their current problems and additionally, by helping them learn problem-solving skills, we decrease the likelihood that these clients will find themselves in need of services in the future. As the information and examples in this chapter have demonstrated, clients who learn to problem-solve feel more empowered, more able to determine for themselves the course of action they need to take, and more competent overall; these all involve the operationalization of key social work values.

CHAPTER 9

INTERVENTION: ADVICE GIVING

With Melisa Atkeson

The nature of social work as a helping profession means that it may attract people who have a passion for helping others solve problems and create better lives. However, one of the pitfalls of this same trait is the tendency toward advice giving. Many times you will have valuable information, advice, and knowledge about services, programs, and resources to share with a client. At times, you may even find yourself tempted to simply tell the client what to do. It is important, however, not to lecture or bombard the client with advice or information, but to engage the client so that the process is collaborative and the client ultimately decides what to do. Our goal as social workers should extend even beyond helping clients to solve their problems; if we successfully include clients in the process, they will begin to understand how to problem-solve for themselves.

Guidelines for providing information are summarized in Exhibit 9.1 and are expanded upon here.

1. First, explore clients' situations and their feelings (Chapters 3 and 4).
2. Ensure that you have elicited clients' own ideas about what they believe they should do.
3. Ask clients about their knowledge of a particular topic and how it applies to them. For example, "You've said you've tried time-out. Tell me about what happened when you did that. Walk me through the steps." This gives people credit for having tried to solve their problem and identifies for the worker the gaps in knowledge that need to be addressed. For instance, if a father says that he used time-out by putting his stepchildren behind the couch for two hours, the worker knows to educate him on the principles of successfully using time-out.
4. Ask the client's permission for you to offer advice by making one of the following types of statements (Miller & Rollnick, 2002):
   - "Would it be all right if I told you a concern I have about what you're proposing to do?"
   - "I have an idea here that may or may not be relevant. Do you want to hear it?"

- "I think I understand your perspective on this. I wonder if it would be okay for me to tell you a few things that occur to me as I listen to you that you might want to consider."
- "There are a few things that may or may not be important to you here, and I want to understand what you think about them before we go on. You probably already know some of these, but I want to make sure. Would that be all right with you?"

5. Acknowledge that the client has the freedom to choose whether or not to accept your advice with the following types of statements (Miller & Rollnick, 2002):
   - "I don't know if this would work for you or not, but I can give you an idea of what some other people have done in your situation."
   - "This is just one possibility. You can decide whether it applies to you."
   - "I can give you an idea, but I think you'd have to try it out to see if it would work for you."

Example: Carmen is a 29-year-old post-partum patient from Latin America being seen at a health clinic. She has been referred to the social work intern because of symptoms of depression. The client mentions that one of her ideas for making money involves selling an herbal supplement product from home like a friend of hers does. In this situation, the social work intern is concerned that the client could be taken advantage of by being co-opted into a pyramid selling scheme and asks permission to share this with the client by saying, "Can I let you know some concerns I have about this?" After permission is granted, the intern could discuss her worry that the client might be persuaded into buying products that she will not be able to sell.

---

6. Offer a cluster of options so the client can choose a course of action from other alternatives (Miller & Rollnick, 2002), making a statement, such as "There's really no one way or right answer. I have some ideas that have worked well for other people, so we can see which one may fit you." This guideline on providing options is also important to keep in mind when referring clients.

From Chapter 7 on goal-setting, recall "Kim," who was given referrals for substance-use treatment. The intern had appropriately offered two options: an outpatient substance-abuse program at the health department that met twice a week and a 28-day inpatient program. Both of these took into account the client's finances and health insurance status and, as such, were viable options.

7. Ensure that any referral or piece of information matches the client's readiness to change.

> **Example:** John is a 47-year-old Caucasian male who was in a county detox program for alcohol withdrawal.
>
> **Intern:** You've been here a few days. What are your plans when you discharge from detox?
>
> **John:** I'm going to go home, to my townhouse. No treatment for me. I've been here a bunch before. I'm fine.
>
> **Intern:** You seem not to be interested in attending treatment.
>
> **John:** No, ma'am. I'm going to go home, start working again. I own my own business, so I can work when I need to. I clean and install air ducts, so I make good money.
>
> **Intern:** What are your plans to help you maintain your sobriety?
>
> **John:** You know, I'm fine.
>
> **Intern:** Do you have a sponsor?
>
> **John:** No.
>
> **Intern:** Have you thought about getting a sponsor or finding out about AA meetings near you?
>
> **John:** Umm . . . I don't know.
>
> **Intern:** If you decide that you would like information on AA meetings near you, we have "Where & When" books available.
>
> **John:** Okay, thanks.

In this situation, the intern talked to the client about getting a sponsor and attending Alcoholics Anonymous meetings, but he is not open to hearing about these options at this time. When people appear unmotivated for change, a better course of action is to switch to motivational interviewing techniques, such as the decisional balance (Chapter 5 or techniques for handling resistance (Chapters 2 and 4). Before making suggestions or offering information, it is vital to assess whether the client is ready to hear it.

8. Once you have offered information and have discussed it with the client, elicit the client's views on how he or she might use the information you have provided. For example, you might say, "Now that we've talked about how you can respond to your child's feelings about the sexual abuse, tell me what you will say when she brings it up."
9. Give feedback in normative terms. An example of this would be: "Many mothers ask why their children didn't come to them about the sexual abuse. There are a lot of reasons children respond that way . . ."
10. Write information down, especially for referrals, so that people can remember important details. People who are overwhelmed often struggle with remembering and implementing the details of a plan. The simple act of writing information down for them will help make things clear.

11. Ask questions so that clients can make their own connections and form their own conclusions. For instance, if a parent says she gives in to her children when they whine, the worker could ask, "What are the consequence of 'giving in?'" and "What do children learn when we give in to whining?" Another lengthier example involves 19-year-old Monique, who lived in foster care. The intern helped Monique apply for financial aid for college, and (in her words) "to also explain the reasons why the Department of Human Services would not allow her to go to a private school in Washington, DC, for college." The exchange below shows the intern's responses. Following that is another version with alternative responses that make the discussion a more collaborative process for imparting information.

Intern: The reason for my visit today is to help you to complete your financial aid, and to also talk to you about Lincoln University.

Monica: Okay.

Intern: So let's talk a little bit about your interest in going to college there. What schools are you interested in, and why Lincoln in particular?

Monica: I've just always wanted to go to Lincoln.

Intern: So it's Lincoln that you are definitely interested in going to?

Monica: Yeah.

Intern: Okay, well I did pull some things about Lincoln off the Internet, like information on admission criteria. I'm not sure what your high school GPA was, but the average GPA is close to a 4.0. And the average SAT score is 1275.

Monica: Yeah, well I got like a 12 something on my SATs.

Intern: Did you? That's great. In addition to the school being competitive, it is also very expensive. Guess how much it costs a year? Do you have any idea?

Monica: No.

Intern: For tuition and room and board, it's about fifty thousand.

Monica: Oh, wow.

Intern: Yeah. There are a ton of other colleges and universities out there that are just as good, and a lot less expensive. Have you looked at any in-state schools?

Monica: No.

Intern: I'd suggest looking at some schools in-state. Also, how many credits are you taking this semester?

Monica: I'm taking two classes.

Intern: So before we even start exploring another college for you, you need to prove to us that you can take on a full load of courses—15 credits—and also do well with that load. We're not going to pay $50,000 for you per year if we don't know you can actually do well. I don't want to disappoint you, but I want to be realistic with you. Does this make sense to you?

Contrast the previous discussion with the one that follows. Look for statements the intern makes that result in a more collaborative exchange.

Intern: The reason for my visit today is to help you to complete your financial aid, and to also talk to you about Lincoln University.

Monica: Okay.

Intern: So let's talk a little bit about your interest in going to college there. What schools are you interested in, and why Lincoln?

Monica: I've just always wanted to go to Lincoln.

Substitute: Tell me what you know about Lincoln.

Monica: Well, it's in DC, which is a city I love, and it has a strong cultural environment that I would like, and you have to work hard.

Substitute: What do you think is the average high school GPA of the people who get in?

Monica: Well it's pretty high, I would guess.

Substitute: And I wonder about SAT scores for getting into Lincoln. What is the average SAT score of students who go there?

Monica: Well, I got like a 12 something on my SATs. I'm not sure what scores they require.

Substitute: We can probably find that out. Let's talk cost for a minute. How much a year is it?

Monica: I don't really know how much it costs.

Substitute: Where do you think you could get both the SAT and the cost information?

Monica: I could maybe look that up on the Internet. Or I could call the school.

Substitute: What in-state schools have you looked at?

Monica: Not too many. Maybe I should look at some of the requirements and costs of other schools in DC and compare them. Even if I want to go to Lincoln, it's good to have a backup.

Substitute: Good idea. Where can you go to find out more about in-state schools?

By prompting the client for information through the use of questions, the social work intern is able to engage the client in the discussion about college. The conversation is no longer the intern's lecture about the expense and educational requirements of the private school; it is a conversation in which Monica must draw on her own knowledge and the resources available to enable her to learn about college requirements.

12. Make material personally relevant.

In the following example, an intern facilitating a foster parent education group was required to do a unit on parenting teenagers. Since this group of foster parents stated that they were not interested in fostering adolescents, the intern had to come up with a way to make the material relevant to the group members, as the following dialogue illustrates.

Leader: How many of you were once a teen? Raise your hand if you were ever a teenager.

(Laughter and raised hands)

Diane: I remember it being a terrible time.

Gail: Yeah, me too. I remember feeling like no one understood me.

Mike: I was really wild.

Leader: All of those are very normal responses to the teen years. Diane, what made it a terrible time for you?

Diane: Other kids were mean to me.

Mike: Ain't that the truth? I think about how mean we were to a couple of kids.

Leader: Mike, what do you think made you behave that way?

Mike: I don't know. We didn't think about it too much. We were just being funny.

Gail: Maybe you were just trying to fit in with a group. Things happen when a group is involved.

Leader: That's a great observation, Gail. It brings up one of the key traits of teen behavior. Anyone have an idea what that might be?

Tanya: Teens want to be just like everyone else. If someone's being mean to someone, they'll just go along with it so they're not different.

Leader: That's exactly right, Tanya. Thanks for sharing that. Social relationships and peers are becoming really important to teens. They're pulling away from their families a little, and friends take on much more importance. What else? Can someone tell me another trait of the "typical" teen? If there is such a thing?

Bianca: They're moody and emotional.

Diane: They're adventurous.

David: Identity. They're trying to figure out who they are.

Emily: They're experimenting. Maybe with drugs or alcohol.

Leader: That's right; teens are establishing their own identity apart from us. So they're playing around with roles to see what seems to fit. Think of it like trying on clothes. They're trying on friends, trying on attitudes, possibly substances, maybe sex; trying on a wide range of new behaviors.

Gail: I remember thinking my parents were so embarrassing. I didn't want to be around them.

Emily: I know! I just wanted to be by myself.

Mike: They're so moody. No one wants to be around them. They don't even like themselves.

Leader: Well, that may be part of it. Teens have to separate from their parents in order to become more independent. It's like two steps forward, one step back, though, because they can't do it all at once. Sometimes they have to think we're idiots in order to "let us go." They need time alone to sort this out.

In this example, the intern tried to normalize teen behavior and to help prospective foster parents remember their own experiences. In this way, she was able to provide information about foster parenting teens without it becoming "a lecture."

13. Ask clients to recall what they know about information that has already been provided to them. Sometimes clients have already been told information; in these cases, repeating it to them might act as a disservice. Once they tell you what they know, you can clarify any misperceptions and fill in any gaps in knowledge.

As an example, an intern was placed in a regional chapter of The Arc, which is a community-based organization of support and services for people with intellectual and developmental disabilities. Mr. and Mrs. Grayson, arriving unexpectedly during the intern's shift, explained that they had an 11-year-old son diagnosed with mild autism. The school had referred them to The Arc to get information about Individualized Education Plans (IEPs) and educational services. At that point, the intern responded, "Since it seems as if you have been involved in your son's IEPs, can you tell me what you already know?"

Mrs. Grayson: I know about the Individuals with Disabilities Education Act and that he is supposed to be provided with services in the least restrictive environment. I just need help in the meetings, and I need people to back me up. They act like I don't know anything.
Intern: You would like someone to go to the meetings with you to help the school understand your point of view?
Mrs. Grayson: Exactly.
Intern: Here at The Arc of Northern Virginia we do have several contacts for educational consultants, and these are people who will go with you to your son's IEP meetings. These educational consultants will also talk to you before the meeting to understand what's going on with the school and specialize in helping families with children with intellectual and/or developmental disabilities.

The mother came in feeling overwhelmed and misunderstood by the school, but the intern's question about what Mrs. Grayson already knew implied that she did possess some knowledge about the services and resources available, likely giving her more confidence. By asking this question, the intern could also begin to clarify this parent's knowledge base in order to target information and referrals more effectively.

Another example involves a social work intern placed at a foster care unit who was assigned to 19-year-old Monica. The intern and the client had already discussed what was required in order for Monica to attend a four-year college the following year. In the next meeting, Monica repeated her desire to attend the four-year college. Rather than going over the requirements again, the social work intern could reference their prior conversation about this topic and explore the client's understanding: "What did we discuss about what needs to happen so you can go to a four-year college?" Monica responds by saying, "This semester I will have a total of 12 credits, so I was wondering, if I do get into one of the schools I apply to for the fall, would I be able to go?" At this point, the social work intern could use another prompt to help Monica recall information provided previously: "Tell me what you remember about what your performance needs to look like." Monica then recites that she will have to pass all her classes, which she is not doing at this time. The conversation can then proceed along the lines of what she can do to improve her performance, rather than a rehash of their previous conversation.

Exercise: In this exercise, the client, Mila, is a 17-year-old mother of a special-needs six-month-old girl. Mila is involved with CPS because of medical neglect. What can the intern do to make her interaction with Mila a more collaborative process?

Intern: I know we have talked about this before, but do you remember what we said needed to happen in order for CPS to close this case?

Mila: Yes, CPS needs to make sure that I am taking my baby to her doctors' appointments.

Intern: Yes, that's the main thing, but we also need to make sure that we see you functioning on your own. For example, making the appointments on your own, keeping up with Medicaid paperwork, getting your baby to her appointments on time, and making sure you leave your baby with an appropriate child care provider.

Mila: Okay.

EXHIBIT 9.1: Guidelines for Imparting Information in a Collaborative Way

Guideline	Application to Your Practice
Explore clients' situations and their feelings.	
Elicit clients own ideas about what they should do.	
Ask clients about their knowledge of a particular topic and how it applies to them.	
Ask the client's permission for you to offer advice.	
Acknowledge the client's freedom to choose to accept the information or not.	
Offer a cluster of options so the client can choose a course of action from alternatives.	
Ensure that any referral or information matches the client's readiness to change.	

Elicit clients' views on how they might use information you have
 provided.
Give feedback in normative terms.
Write down important information.
Ask questions that help clients make their own connections and
 form their own conclusions.
Make material personally relevant.
Reference prior information provided to the client.

EXERCISE FOR YOUR PRACTICE

Take each of the guidelines in Exhibit 9.1 and, based on your agency's purpose and
tasks, apply how you would use these guidelines at your setting.

CONCLUSION

Because of your knowledge and expertise, you will often have information and resources
that can be of great use to people who find themselves in extremely difficult situations. This
chapter has continued the theme of collaboration in that even referrals and information can
be presented in a way that is respectful, takes advantage of people's readiness to receive such
information, and empowers them to act as the experts on themselves and to utilize resources
effectively. In this manner, collaborative information-giving enacts and balances two of
social work's core values—service and the dignity and worth of the person.

CHAPTER 10

INTERVENTION: IMPLEMENTING THE PLAN AND HANDLING LACK OF COMPLIANCE

After you and your clients have collaboratively come up with ideas for what they can do to change their behavior or a situation, you will have to work with them to figure out how they will actually implement their plan in practice and to manage any challenges that they encounter. Motivating clients to take ownership of their change plans in a way that empowers and respects them is the topic of this chapter.

DEVELOPING THE PLAN

When clients are considering ideas for changes, your role entails talking through all the steps involved, as well as the possible challenges and obstacles. For example, if you have given a client a referral for a certain resource or service, you can ask them, "What will you ask for when you call?" "What will you say?" "What if the person you need to talk to is unavailable?"

Recall the example of Seth, the six-year-old boy in foster care. He and the intern came up with the options of "telling the teacher" and "ignoring" another child's annoying behaviors rather than reacting physically. Let's say Seth decided to go with the option of telling the teacher. The intern can explore implementation of the plan by asking, "How will you tell the teacher?" "What words will you use? What do you think will happen next?" The intern could also ask about potential barriers that may be involved in his plan, such as "What might other kids say if you tell the teacher?" The task here is to help people consider the details of their plan and help them work through the steps that will be necessary so that their good ideas will have sufficient chance to succeed.

Exercise: In Chapter 8, the example of Rita appeared in which she decided that the best recourse for her troublesome relationship with her daughter was to ignore and avoid her. How would you discuss implementing this plan with the client?

ROLE PLAYING

In addition to discussing the details of the client's plans for change, role playing can be enormously helpful in assisting people to practice new behaviors. One of the core values of social work is the importance of human relationships. Role-plays help people practice new interpersonal behaviors so that they are more effective at influencing their environment and fostering healthy relationships.

In order to have an effective role-play, the following guidelines from Hepworth et al. (2010) should be considered:

1. Define a problem that has to do with an interactional pattern that the client wants to change. That is, role playing is useful when the client's problem has to do with an interaction between two or more people.
2. Discuss how the client can handle a difficult interpersonal situation. Educate on communication skills, if needed. See Exhibit 10.1.
3. Give the client the rationale for a role-play by making a statement such as, "We have talked about how you can handle this situation, but it is actually much more effective if you can practice the behavior. Would you be willing to do a role-play with me? This way you get to practice the new behavior in a safe environment before actually doing it."
4. Model the skills so clients can observe the new behavior first before they have to try it. Clients are often nervous, since it means that they will be trying out new or uncomfortable behaviors, but you can reassure them that you will be modeling the behavior first.

EXHIBIT 10.1: **Steps to Teach Clients Communication Skills**

---

1. Relay why communication skills are important:
   - to initiate new relationships
   - to build or maintain already-existing relationships
   - to experience closeness with others
   - to state feelings and reactions to let others know of their influence and to get them to act more positively
   - to cope with feelings by sharing them with others
2. Teach reflective listening.
   Explain what reflective listening means: paraphrasing the content of the speaker's message and one's perceptions of the underlying feelings in order to convey understanding of the person's message. To do this, use the basic format: "What I hear you saying . . ." or "You seem to be feeling . . . [*mad, sad, scared, glad*] because [*give brief reason*]." Generally, the most difficulty people have with this technique is understanding that reflective listening does not mean they necessarily agree with the speaker's message. Rather, it conveys understanding to ensure that the other person feels heard.
3. Teach "I" messages.
   Present the basic format: *I feel* (personal reactions) to *what happened* (a specific activating event).
4. Ask people to change their behavior.
   Sometimes when people use "I" messages, they want nothing more than to be heard. At other times, however, they would like others to change their behavior. Behavior requests should be behaviorally specific, measurable, and stated as the presence of positive behaviors (i.e., "Please be home at six o'clock for dinner" rather than "Stop being late all the time").

---

5. Discuss how the modeling went ("What do you think? How was that different from what usually happens or what you thought might happen?"). You can also offer some empathy for the client's situation after assuming his or her role: "I see that she can be very persistent in getting you to change your mind. What did I do to make sure she got the message?"

6. The client rehearses the new skill: Do the role-play again, this time having the client practice the new behavior as him- or herself. After having taken part in the first phase of the role-play, clients are usually quick to pick up on the new behavior. Sometimes, when first asserting themselves in this new role, they may become emotional and teary as well. If this happens, you can commend them on working through their emotions in the role-play, pointing out that they will be better equipped to handle the situation in real life. The rehearsal process enables parts of the skill that were unclear or that were misunderstood to come to light for clarification and also enhances the client's confidence that the skill can be generalized to a real-life situation.

7. The client and practitioner process the behavioral rehearsal. The client expresses what it was like to try on the new behavior. The practitioner offers compliments on areas that went well and feedback for improvement, if necessary. At this point, the client may be offered another opportunity to rehearse.

The following scenario offers the opportunity to look at a role-play in more detail to help you maximize the effectiveness of this technique. After you read the dialogue below, decide what went well and what you would do differently.

Belinda (age 40) has a severe mental illness (schizoaffective disorder) and resides in a supported living program. Belinda has talked about feeling more depressed recently, and the staff have noticed weight loss and withdrawal. Belinda attributes her depression to her feelings of intimidation in regard to one of her three housemates. The following dialogue illustrates the situation and the role-play the intern initiates:

Belinda: She just asks too much of us. We want to help because we are her friends and it's really hard to see a friend like that, but we can't always be doing the things she's asking us to do.

Intern: What kinds of things does she ask you to do?

Belinda: Well, this weekend when she came home from the hospital she expected us to wait on her hand and foot. She needed this, she needed that, and she wanted us to bring things to her. She asked me to make her food, and she asked the others the same things.

Intern: So it sounds like you're torn because Eliza is a friend, but you also feel that she is taking advantage of you and expects you to do too much for her.

Belinda: Right, and it's just so hard because none of us are assertive people. We don't know how to say "no." We just can't say no.

Intern: Assertiveness is something that is hard for a lot of people to express. It can be very difficult to say "no," especially to a friend.

Belinda: Yeah, it's very hard.

Intern: I have an idea. I hear you saying that assertiveness is something you want to work on, so maybe we could try something called a role-play. It would give you some practice being assertive.

Belinda: How do you do it?

Intern: First you would be the person you want to be assertive to, and I will play you. Then we will switch, so that you are you and I am the person to whom you want to be assertive. Does that make sense?

Belinda: Yes. I think so.

Intern: Let's try it. What situation do you want to practice?

Belinda: One with Eliza. How about one of the phone calls she makes asking me for things?

Intern: That sounds like a good idea. Ready?

Belinda: I think so.

Intern: Remember, I'm you and you are Eliza.

Belinda: Okay . . . Ring ring.

Intern as Belinda: Hello, this is Belinda.

Belinda as Eliza: Hey, Miss America!

Intern as Belinda: Hi, Eliza. How are you feeling?

Belinda as Eliza: I'm not so good. This hospital is driving me crazy.

Belinda: I don't know if I can do this.

Intern: You're doing a great job so far.

Belinda: Okay . . . um.

Intern as Belinda: I'm sorry to hear that the hospital is driving you crazy.

Belinda as Eliza: Yeah, it is. So I was wondering, do you know where my meds are? I'm so mad I left them at home.

Intern as Belinda: Yes, they are sitting on the china cabinet right here.

Belinda as Eliza: Good. Belinda, I really need you to bring them to me.

Intern as Belinda: I'm sorry Eliza, but I can't do that.

Belinda: Now what do I say?

Intern: What would Eliza say?

Belinda as Eliza: Why not?

Intern as Belinda: I have some things planned for today and don't have time to stop by the hospital.

Belinda as Eliza: You call yourself a friend? Some friend! You can't even find time to come by and bring me my meds? Don't you even care about me?

Intern as Belinda: Of course we're friends. I just can't come by the hospital today. Maybe you can ask one of the nurses if they can help you out with your med situation. Hope you feel better, Eliza. Goodbye.

Belinda: (laughing) I don't know if I could do that.

Intern: It sounds like she tries to make you feel guilty.

Belinda: Yep.

Intern: Well, I think that was a great first attempt at role playing. What do you think?

Belinda: Yeah, it was okay.

Intern: All right, now let's switch roles.

Belinda: Oh, right.

Intern: Ring ring.

Belinda as herself: Hello?

Intern as Eliza: Belinda, it's Eliza! Guess what? I just got discharged from the hospital again! I'm going to need a ride home. Can you come get me?

Belinda as herself: No, Eliza, I'm sorry I can't.

Intern as Eliza: Why can't you?

Belinda as herself: I actually have plans and I'm already on my way out the door.

Intern as Eliza: But how am I supposed to get home? I really need a ride home!

Belinda as herself: I'm sorry, but I can't give you a ride. Maybe someone else will be able to. Goodbye.

Intern: That was good, Belinda. What did you think about the whole process?

Belinda: It's kind of hard. I still don't know if I could really do it.

Intern: It can be very difficult to say "no" to people, especially friends. But with practice it may become easier. We can continue to work on assertiveness in future meetings if it is something you'd like to work on.

Belinda: It is.

For this example, we will make the assumption that the intern knew the client well enough to determine at the outset that role playing was an appropriate technique to use given the interactional problems with the housemate. It is unclear, however, how much time the intern spent educating the client on basic assertiveness skills, such as the use of "I" messages. There also could have been more discussion with the client at various junctures. After the intern modeled the skills, she could have asked Belinda how this behavior might be difficult or different for her, and she could have asked about any perceived obstacles. After the client rehearsed the communication skills, the intern then could have asked what the client's experience was like. Indeed, the client made a direct statement, "I don't know if I could really do this," so the intern could have explored this further. If it turned out that the client was still not confident in her ability to have a successful interaction, the intern could have offered the client another opportunity to practice the skill. Since the situation seems important to the client, and the client has indicated that she feels motivated to keep working on it, saving it for another time seems unnecessary.

Exercise: In the following situation at a long-term retirement community, the client, Mrs. Hastings, and the intern have agreed that going to church services might be a way for the client to both improve her mood and to become more involved in the retirement community. When the client expresses worry that she won't know how to follow along, the intern has explored with her the idea of asking another person present for help. How can you make a role-play such as this one more effective?

Intern: Let's role-play. I'm one of the church ladies, Mrs. Smith, and I'm sitting all by myself before the service begins with my bulletin in my lap and ready to worship. So, you come up to me and what do you say?
Mrs. Hastings: Hi, I'm Donna Hastings. How are you?
Intern as Mrs. Smith: I'm fine, thanks, I'm Mrs. Smith.
Mrs. Hastings: Can I sit here?
Intern as Mrs. Smith: Sure.
Mrs. Hastings: (Silence)
Intern: Ok, now this is where you could ask me about following along.
Mrs. Hastings: Can you help me follow along with the service? Sometimes I don't hear well and get confused about where we are.
Intern as Mrs. Smith: Sure, I would be glad to . . .
Intern: So was that hard for you to do?
Mrs. Hastings: No, I think I could do that.
Intern: Good. I look forward to hearing how it goes when you go to the church service this Sunday.

Role-plays can be successfully used with many different types of client situations: romantic breakups, handling children's misbehavior, refusing an unreasonable request, or advocating for services and resources. Many social workers utilize role-plays because they help the client change by practicing new behavior in a safe environment. By doing so, clients are much better prepared to generalize their new skills to actual situations.

EXERCISE FOR YOUR PRACTICE

For what client situation would a role-play be an appropriate technique? How would you approach doing a role-play in this situation? What exactly would you say?

HANDLING LACK OF COMPLIANCE

Although ideas, goals, and tasks may have been decided with client input, you are probably not surprised to find that clients may not follow through with agreed-upon plans. Consider how hard it is to change our own behavior, such as overeating or watching too much TV. We may start out with the best of intentions, only to have them dissolve in the face of stressful situations, temptation, or simply the effort it takes to move out of a familiar pattern of behavior.

When clients fail to follow through, we can still maintain a collaborative stance rather than lecturing, scolding, or shaming them. You can explore with the client, in a neutral and nonjudgmental manner, the reasons for the lack of follow-through. Being nonjudgmental does not mean failing to address the client's behavior or letting it go by saying, "Oh, it's okay." This would give the message that the work you have helped them with is unimportant, and the client might lose motivation and become similarly dismissive.

Instead, at the next meeting with the client, inquire about the completion of the task, spending at least five minutes discussing the outcome to emphasize the importance of following through on what was decided (Carroll, 1998). If a person was unable to do the assigned task, time should be spent discussing what got in the way and negotiating the task for the following week. It could be, for instance, that the task was too ambitious for the client and needs to be broken down into smaller, more manageable pieces.

See Exhibit 10.2 for a summary of steps to handle noncompliance.

Strategy	Application

1. Check in at next contact after a client task has been agreed upon.
2. Use open-ended questions to explore with the client his or her understanding of the task.
3. Discuss any reasons for noncompliance, using select questions as a guide:[1]
   • What makes this hard for you to do?
   • What can you do to make it easier for you to complete the assignment this week?
   • What assignment might be more useful for you?
   • What thoughts come to mind when you think about this assignment?
   • Does this seem relevant?
   • How could we make this more helpful?
4. Role-play if the task involves an interpersonal situation.
5. Renegotiate the task, asking the person to summarize what has been agreed upon.

[1] Webster-Stratton & Herbert (1993)

EXERCISES

Exercise 1: In the scenario that follows, the intern worked in a mental health facility that was set up as semi-independent living. One of her clients was a 49-year-old Hispanic woman, Ms. Velasquez, who was recovering from a leg fracture when she fell in the snow and broke her knee. She spent some time in the hospital but is now living in the facility again. What would you do differently in this instance? What specifically would you say?

Intern: Hi, Ms. Velasquez.

Ms. Velasquez: Hi. C'mon over and have a seat.

Intern: I'm glad I found you. I stopped by earlier.

Ms. Velasquez: I was there a little while ago, but left to have a cigarette.

Intern: How is your knee?

Ms. Velasquez: It's much better than last week.

Intern: How was your physical therapy yesterday?

Ms. Velasquez: I didn't go. The taxi cab came over to pick me up for the therapy, but I wasn't feeling well.

Intern: This is the third time you have missed the session. What makes it hard for you to attend the sessions?

Ms. Velasquez: Nothing. I will go next week.

Intern: That is what you have been saying for the past three weeks, but you don't go.

Exercise 2: Natalia is a 19-year-old Hispanic female who entered the foster care system when she was removed from an abusive home. Natalia attends an apartment-based independent living program that helps foster care youth transition from residential care to independent living. In the following scenario, how can the intern maintain a collaborative relationship with the client and avoid being accusatory?

Intern: So where have you been?
Natalia: What do you mean?
Intern: You haven't been around when we stop by to see you.
Natalia: What are you talking about? I've been here.
Intern: When we have stopped by we've been leaving notes.
Natalia: I know. I got those.
Intern: But the thing is Natalia, you haven't been home at night.
Natalia: What do you mean?
Intern: You are supposed to be home by curfew, and the night staff has been by to check up on you at five a.m. and you weren't home.
Natalia: Oh, yeah, but that only happened twice.
Intern: So where have you been?
Natalia: I've been taking care of my son at his grandma's house' cause everyone is at work.
Intern: Is that why you missed your meeting with your social worker and driving instructor last week?
Natalia: Yeah, but I called my social worker.
Intern: Your social worker and I have talked. And right now you are on discharge status because you haven't been participating in the program.
Natalia: What does that mean?
Intern: Since you haven't been home for curfew checks and haven't participated in groups, you will probably be kicked out of the program.
Natalia: I'm going to participate now. It was just last week that I had to watch my son' cause no one could watch him.
Intern: Why couldn't you call?
Natalia: I called my social worker and left her a message.
Intern: But why didn't you tell me? If you had called me, we could have given you a pass so you could watch your son.

Exercise 3: Habiba is a single Muslim female client with four children who has been in the transitional housing program for three months. The client is currently not in compliance with her agreement to find employment or a volunteer situation, and she has missed a required life-skills class. How can the intern avoid lecturing the client and instead foster a collaborative relationship with her?

Intern: Hello, Habiba.

Habiba: Hi.

Intern: Hello (to Habiba's son).

The son gives a silent and angry stare.

Intern: You have been in the program for three months now, right?

Habiba: Yes.

Intern: As you know, our policy states that you must be working, volunteering, or taking classes. After three months of noncompliance, we issue what is called a 21/30, which states that the noncompliance must be corrected within 21 days or you must vacate the premises within 30 days. Additionally, you missed your life-skills class this week.

Habiba: Yes, I cannot find a job and I have been busy taking my son to and from school. I was sick last week at the time of life-skills class.

Intern: If you are sick, you must provide us with a doctor's excuse, because three unexcused absences will cause you to be terminated from the program. Why is your son not taking the bus to school?

Habiba: He refuses to ride the bus.

Intern: Why? You need to be looking for work and attending life-skills classes, not transporting him to school.

Habiba: He will not go to school otherwise.

Intern: Where have you applied for jobs?

Habiba: I applied at Giant and Safeway.

Intern: Have you called them back to follow up on your application? You need to step up your search.

Habiba: No.

Intern: You need to do this. What kind of work do you want to do?

Habiba: Cashier, but I do not know if I can do this because of my back.

Intern: Perhaps, you should start by volunteering as a cashier. This way you can see if you can do this kind of work. We can also help you further your education. Do you have your high school diploma?

Habiba: Yes, I have a diploma from my country.

Intern: I know that you have met with the employment counselor and you have recently completed your résumé. If you begin doing volunteer work, then you can spend your off hours in our office with the employment specialist looking for work.

Exercise 4: In the example below, foster parents Tara and Chris have been able to help their foster child improve her behaviors. However, they do not always comply with the Department of Human Services' rules and policies. They have missed several therapy appointments without calling or e-mailing to say they can't attend, and they do not complete weekly foster parent logs and some of the other necessary paperwork. The intern's purpose for the contact is to discuss with the foster parents their lack of completing the logs. How could you approach the issue with the foster parent in a more collaborative way?

Intern: I wanted to talk to you about the foster parent logs.
Chris: Okay.
Intern: We discussed at the last treatment team meeting the importance of completing one detailed foster parent log or two shorter foster parent logs each week. We haven't received any foster parent logs for the past month.
Chris: I remember. I've just been really busy and sometimes I forget.
Intern: I understand that it can be difficult to find the time, but it is important to complete them every week.

EXERCISE FOR YOUR PRACTICE

Have you encountered a situation in which a client has not followed through with an agreed-upon plan? How can you handle this using the guidelines listed in Exhibit 10.2 and the material from this chapter?

CLOSING AND OPENING CONTACTS WITH CLIENTS

There are ways to maximize the effectiveness of the endings and beginnings of subsequent sessions. Ending the session involves getting closure, evaluation of the contact, and planning for next time. Exhibit 10.3 discusses these points, along with examples. You are also asked to consider how a contact you recently observed or carried out yourself ended (or could have ended) using these strategies. Similarly, Exhibit 10.4 offers guidelines for starting up subsequent sessions (Miller & Rollnick, 2002).

CONCLUSION

Implementing the plan is a critically important stage of the helping process. This is the stage where you help clients take action to solve their problems and change their situations. The examples in this chapter have hopefully shown you that when implementing an agreed-upon plan, it is critical to discuss in detail the steps involved, as well as the potential obstacles that may arise. This may also happen when the client, for one reason or another, fails to implement the plan. It is important to avoid becoming punitive and lecturing clients at these times and instead discuss any noncompliance in a respectful and collaborative way that places ownership on the client. Finally, role playing has been offered as an excellent way to operationalize the core social work value of human relationships and to help people practice new behaviors that they can then enact in their lives.

PART 5

EVALUATION AND TERMINATION

CHAPTER 11

EVALUATION AND TERMINATION

The final stage of the helping process is termination and evaluation. This chapter covers preparation for termination and the tasks involved with this final phase of our collaborative relationship with a client. Also discussed is a way to handle non-planned terminations in a way that emphasizes and reinforces client strengths.

PREPARATION FOR TERMINATION

Social workers must plan for termination and prepare clients for it in advance. Indeed, appropriate termination is listed as an ethical responsibility to clients in the NASW Code of Ethics (1999). As well as allowing people to prepare for termination emotionally, the prospect of a time limit can motivate people toward their goals. In your internship, it is likely that you will have the opportunity to terminate with clients. This may occur even before the client work is finished, as your internship has a definite end date. An example of preparing for termination with a client might look like the following: "As we've talked about, I have only four weeks left at my internship. What would you like to accomplish before I leave?"

TASKS OF TERMINATION

The termination process involves three tasks: 1) evaluation of the work, 2) processing feelings attached to the termination, and 3) making plans for the future.

EVALUATION

Evaluation comprises discussion of clients' progress toward goals and their accomplishments during the period you have worked with them: "Tell me how your life is different since we started working together." "What have you been able to accomplish?" Evaluation also involves discussing what has instigated change and what has been helpful in the process of change: "What did we do here that you felt made a difference?" "What was most helpful?" "What was least helpful?" These questions imply that clients are their own experts on the change process. They also empower them to take credit for this change.

PROCESSING FEELINGS

The second task of the ending stage is to focus on clients' feelings about termination and separation. People may have a range of feelings toward ending their work with you: sadness, excitement for the future, anger that you are leaving. Some people act unconcerned, as if the period of time you have spent together has meant nothing to them. In these cases, you may assume that they are having some difficulty with the termination process, and you may want to bring their reaction to light: "I notice that you're shrugging off the importance of what we have worked on together. Is that a typical reaction when you're saying goodbye?" Since dealing with difficult losses may have been a part of a client's history, sometimes your termination will trigger these feelings of loss. Discussing previous life events around loss may be appropriate at these times.

Termination with you may also be a way for clients to have what is called a "corrective experience around loss." For the first time, a client may have the chance to express feelings and process the emotions and the work rather than be faced with an abrupt or unprocessed leave-taking such as those that have been inflicted on him or her in the past.

You may also experience emotional reactions when you terminate with clients. Here are some of the possibilities: satisfaction about the work you have done together; pride that your client has progressed so well; relief that you are seeing the last of a challenging client; sadness that you are letting go of a meaningful relationship and/or in reaction to your client's sadness; disappointment that more wasn't achieved; or fear about how a client will fare in the future. Not all of these reactions will be shared with the client, but it is important to recognize and acknowledge them in yourself and to discuss them in supervision.

BUILDING ON CHANGE

A third task of termination involves *discussion* of the ways people can *maintain and continue their growth* as they generalize their learning to everyday challenges. Termination is geared toward helping clients identify strategies so their changes will be maintained and the momentum developed will continue to promote desired progress.

Part of termination, therefore, is to help clients prevent against relapse of harmful behaviors, such as substance use, anger problems, or association with unhealthy relationships. The client must be prepared with strategies to enact if temptation presents itself or if he or she begins to slip into old behaviors. Recall that we talked about the use of solution-focused language and its implication that positive change is a certainty. However, during termination, you want to use what's called possibility, or tentative, phrasing: "What *would* be the first thing you'd notice *if* you started to find things slipping back?" "What *could* you do to prevent things from going any further?" "*If* you have the urge to drink again, what *could* you do to make sure you didn't use?" The questions are phrased in a tentative fashion for two reasons. The first reason is to avoid prescribing that relapse is inevitable. The second is to get clients to consider what might be warning signals and what they can do in the event that these signals occur. In this way, they protect themselves against a return to old behavior.

Additionally, termination involves maintaining change ("After you leave here, what will you be doing to keep things going in the direction you want?") and building on the changes that have occurred ("In the future, what will indicate to you that these changes are continuing to happen?") (Bertolino & O'Hanlon, 2002, p. 224). Questions are phrased to set up the expectation that change will continue to happen, that it is a process that can occur even though you are no longer working together.

Social workers must further ensure that there are linkages to continued needed supports (Rooney & Chovanec, 2004) and that clients are informed about changes in workers. If there is the opportunity, it is good practice to offer a period of time for a new worker to overlap with you so that there is a transition period between your leaving and the new worker starting. This provides continuity for the client and allows the new worker to gain a window into the relationship the client has had with you. Exhibit 11.1 summarizes the termination process.

EXHIBIT 11.1: Termination

What is useful?
- What strategies have you learned that have been particularly helpful?
- What strategy did you find least helpful? How would you change it so that it could be more helpful for you? What would you uncover if you'd done it this way?

Momentum
- As you continue making these changes, what will you be doing in six months?

Prevention
- What *would* be the first thing you'd notice *if* you started to find yourself slipping back into depression?
- What *could* you do to prevent depression from setting in any further?

Linkage and support

EXAMPLE

Sometimes, interns themselves have difficulty with the prospect of the client relationship ending, and in an effort to "lessen the blow" they gloss over it, or minimize the fact that it is happening. The following is an example of how *not* to terminate with a client.

Identify the problems evident in the brief scenario below. Then, contrast the first scenario with the one that follows it, which better illustrates how termination could have been approached much more effectively.

The intern is nearing the end of her time with a non-profit agency that provides mental health services to teens and young adults. The client is Julia, a 24-year-old Caucasian female who has been working voluntarily with the intern for six months. Julia had symptoms of depression, which caused her to lose her job due to excessive absences. This, in turn, resulted in her having to move out of the apartment she shared with three other young women and move back in with her parents.

> **Intern:** So, I wanted to let you know that after next week, I'm going to be leaving Family Connections and won't be working with you anymore.
>
> **Julia:** So what will happen to me?
>
> **Intern:** Well, you'll have another worker. I'm sure the agency will find someone good for you to work with.
>
> **Julia:** What if I don't like the new worker?
>
> **Intern:** Then it would be important for you to be honest about that and to tell the supervisor so they can try to make it work. Okay, so let's talk some more about what we were working on last week.
>
> **Julia:** I don't remember what we were talking about.
>
> **Intern:** Well, we were discussing the plan for you to move out of your parents' house and live on your own again.
>
> **Julia:** Yeah, but I don't think I want to do that anymore.
>
> **Intern:** What caused you to change your mind?

Contrast the excerpt above with the following. What is done well in this example?

> **Intern:** So, Julia, do you remember when we first started working together we talked about how at the end of my internship I would be leaving?
>
> **Julia:** Yes, I remember, we've talked about it a few times.
>
> **Intern:** Well, I wanted to remind you that we have about another month together, and to talk about what the plan is after I go.
>
> **Julia:** Okay, so what will happen?
>
> **Intern:** Next week I'm going to be bringing the worker who will take over for me to our meeting so you can meet her and we can talk together about the great progress you're making.
>
> **Julia:** Do you know her?
>
> **Intern:** I've worked with her at the agency. But it will be great for the three of us to have time together, maybe a couple of sessions. I'll get to know her better, and so will you. You can share with her whatever you'd like while I'm still here.
>
> **Julia:** What will she want me to work on?
>
> **Intern:** Well, remember, your goals are your own. You have the ability to decide what you want to do. You've done such a great job since we've been working together. Tell me what changes you've made.
>
> **Julia:** Well, let's see. I got a job that I really like, and I don't feel nearly as unhappy as I did when we first started working together.

Intern: What helped you do that?

Julia: One thing is that now I can tell when I start to feel lonely and I can reach out to friends to go do stuff.

Intern: And what else?

Julia: Well, I've been able to keep my job because I'm not missing work because of feeling sad.

Intern: So those things are huge. And you've really worked hard on the plan we came up with. You've done things that weren't naturally comfortable for you, and it's really paid off. I know that you're going to use the things you've learned to make the other changes you want.

Julia: Yeah, I guess I will be able to.

Intern: So, if it's okay with you, we'll spend the rest of the time today talking about how things are going at home and your plan for moving out of your parents' house.

Julia: Okay.

In the second scenario, it was obvious that the intern had spent time preparing Julia that their time together would end. There was planning and preparation involved, and Julia will have the opportunity to make the transition without feeling abandoned. The intern outlines the progress that Julia has made so far and presents the likelihood that she will continue to use what she has learned to move forward with other changes. Julia is able to hear this information and to move on to talk about the work they are currently doing together, as opposed to the first scenario, in which the information about termination had taken her by surprise and seemed to have short-circuited the work.

EXERCISES

Exercise 1: Risa was not receiving appropriate experience and supervision for a first-year masters student at her internship, so the decision by her school of social work's field department was to transfer Risa to another agency for the second semester. On the last day of her field placement at the residential home where she worked with women afflicted with severe mental illness, she said goodbye and talked about her transfer. The intern was surprised that the women expressed shock and sadness that she was leaving. Risa said she had not expected that reaction since she didn't think the work she was doing at the home was that meaningful.

What are your thoughts about how the termination process was handled here?

Exercise 2: A 17-year-old female resident of a group home had been previously abandoned by her parents and was now in a group home. This particular day, she had discovered "out of the blue" that she was getting a new social worker and that she would be at the group home longer than anticipated. She was noticeably upset in the morning, but as the day wore on she became unresponsive and was found lying on the floor staring with glazed eyes. At one point she lashed out at another resident, tearing at her clothing.

What are your thoughts about how the termination process was handled here?

EXERCISES FOR YOUR PRACTICE

Exercise 1: In preparation for termination, consider the client you have worked with the longest and discuss how you will handle the three tasks of termination.

1.
2.
3.

Exercise 2: What are your emotional reactions in terminating with your clients? Which of these are appropriate to share with your clients? Which are appropriate to share only in supervision?

HANDLING UNPLANNED TERMINATIONS

Sometimes you will not have the opportunity to go through these tasks of termination because a client leaves services abruptly. These are called unplanned terminations. There are a variety of reasons for their occurrence, such as instability in a client's life, disinterest in pursuing change, anxiety about change, or the client's having gotten what he or she wanted out of the change process.

One way to handle this type of termination, especially when a client withdraws from services before the agreed-upon time period, is to write the person a letter. White and Epston (1990) have discussed the importance of narrative methods, particularly letter writing, to emphasize client strengths. Many agencies send out form letters to clients who terminate prematurely. Practitioners may consider revising such a letter to add a strengths-based portion. This portion would act to affirm clients' resources and successes and to highlight the goals clients have for their lives and the progress they have made thus far. If a client is involuntary, the practitioner may want to compliment the person for the courage to approach services and to explore and consider change. As these approaches illustrate, the practitioner should strive to end on a positive note, emphasizing the positive goals clients have for themselves and the wisdom they have for making choices that are in their best interest.

As an example, the following is a letter to a Spanish-speaking immigrant student, Alicia, age 13, written when the intern who worked in Alicia's school left her placement.

> Dear Alicia:
> I enjoyed working with you this year. It was great to see the effort you put into each session and how your grades in all your classes improved as a result. You were able to talk to your teachers for clarification of your assignments, and you took the initiative of going to your counselor to change your math class. These were excellent strategies to use that you can continue next year: talking to your teachers about your assignments and ensuring that your class schedule fits for you. Although I am not going to be here next year at your school, there will be other people working in this program that will be happy to help you.
> Best to you,
> Marlene Fischer

Another example involves a letter written by an intern placed at a child protective services system. The intern had been working on an ongoing basis with Mr. Lange, who had been physically abusive to his children but had been living apart from them since the investigation.

> Dear Mr. Lange:
> I know how much your family means to you and how motivated that has made you to work on managing the anger. Your hard work has paid off—you have made it all the way to the "Third-Party Supervision" step, only one step away from full reunification.
> I hope that you will continue to attend your group, manage the anger, and continue to support your wife and children, as you have demonstrated during our time together. It's not always easy to make responsible decisions, but I, and the others here at CPS, know you have that ability because you have shown it on a weekly basis. I am proud of your accomplishments.
> As you know, my internship with child protective services is ending, but you may continue to communicate any concerns, questions, or comments to [_____] as you did before I joined you. Thank you for the opportunity to work with you, and best to you and your family.
> Regards,
> Robert Hatcher

These types of letters are an obvious improvement to generic termination letters that are often generated by social service agencies. They add a personal dimension to the termination process that conveys a sense of caring. They leave the client with a positive impression about intervention, which hopefully will allow him or her to utilize services again in the future, if warranted. Such letters are an intervention in themselves, highlighting goals, progress, and accomplishments, and may be kept by clients as encouragement to continue positive change.

EXERCISE FOR YOUR PRACTICE

Have you experienced an unplanned termination from a client? If so, craft a letter, perhaps using your agency form letter as a starting point, and add the strengths-based elements that have been discussed here.

CONCLUSION

All of our relationships with clients will have a beginning, a middle, and an end. In order for the end, the termination phase, to be as successful as possible, social workers should begin to discuss it early in the client relationship. Many clients come for help because they have experienced grief, loss, or difficulties with interpersonal relationships. We have a responsibility to clients to make sure that our work with them is terminated in a way that leaves them feeling enabled and empowered to exist in the world without us, and doesn't compound any previous negative experiences of loss. Not only does how we terminate with clients affect the end of our work with them, but it can have a significant impact on how they feel about future relationships and work with others.

PART 6

ETHICS

CHAPTER 12

OPERATIONALIZING ETHICS

With William Hayden and Melisa Atkeson

The NASW Code of Ethics (1999) establishes the basic *values, ethical principles,* and *ethical standards* of the field. What are the differences between these three concepts?

- A *value* is a simple statement about what is important to social workers.
- A *principle* is a general directive that describes how social workers act in accordance with this value.
- A *standard* is a longer statement of the social worker's ethical responsibilities to clients, colleagues, practice settings, professionals, the profession, and society as a whole. Standards provide detailed and specific language about professional conduct.

Because ethics and values are fairly abstract notions, this chapter will detail how these can be operationalized in specific client situations that have relevance to beginning practitioners. You will recognize some of the scenarios from other parts of the book, but in this chapter you will evaluate them from the standpoint of social work values and ethics. In some of the examples posed, the social workers or interns proceed in an ethical manner; in others, the values, principles, or standards are in question. In the latter situations, options are then posed about how the practitioner may act in a more ethical fashion. As well as reading examples, you will develop your knowledge of ethics by reviewing and exploring the ethics from various scenarios that have been drawn from real-life practice situations. At the end of the chapter, you can reflect on circumstances that arise in your own practice.

VALUES AND PRINCIPLES

Exhibit 12.1 presents the social work values, along with their supporting principles. The value of *service* is foundational to all that we do as social workers. The supporting principle

Service	*Social workers' primary goal is to help people in need and to address social problems.*
Social Justice	*Social workers challenge social injustice.*
Dignity and Worth of the Person	*Social workers respect the inherent dignity and worth of the person.*
Importance of Human Relationships	*Social workers recognize the central importance of human relationships.*
Integrity	*Social workers behave in a trustworthy manner.*
Competence	*Social workers practice within their areas of competence and develop and enhance their professional expertise.*

Source: NASW Code of Ethics (1999)

is that we help people in need and address social problems. You will see throughout the chapter how this value arises in every situation we encounter.

As social workers, we seek *social justice*, another prime value. Susan, a student intern at a senior activity center, discovered that one of her clients, Ms. Roberts, a 72-year-old African American woman, suffered from bedbug infestation at her Section 8 apartment. Ms. Roberts had contacted her landlord several times about this problem. Twice he informed her that exterminators would come to her apartment, but on both occasions, they did not show up. The intern helped Ms. Roberts write a letter of complaint to her landlord demanding that he provide a pest-control service to make her apartment habitable. In the letter, the intern not only detailed the attempts Ms. Roberts had made to resolve the problem, she also cited relevant standards of Section 8 housing policies and Department of Health codes.

According to the value of *social justice*, social workers must advocate for social change, particularly with and on behalf of vulnerable and oppressed people. In this situation, Ms. Roberts is elderly, impoverished, and a member of an ethnic minority group. As she has been ignored by the landlord and continues to have an infestation problem, the intern, operating under the value of social justice, intervenes on behalf of the client.

Another central social work value involves the *dignity and worth of all human beings*. Recall from Chapter 10 Habiba, a single Muslim female client living with her four children in a transitional housing program. The client was not in compliance with her agreement to find employment or volunteer work, and she had missed her required life-skills class. However, rather than lecturing Habiba, the social worker could demonstrate *the value of the dignity and worth of the person* by listening to her and conveying understanding. The social worker could find a way to impart information about the requirements of the program and work with (rather than against) the client in finding solutions. (A way to accomplish this is provided in Chapter 10)

A fourth salient value for the social work profession is the *importance of human relationships*; that is, we enhance relationships in a person's environment (the family, other social group, or community). We also use our relationships with our clients as a vehicle for change. A social worker in a juvenile offender community monitoring program spoke with a sobbing 13-year-old Latino who told her about his mother hitting him on numerous occasions. He said there were no marks or bruises, but clearly it was very emotionally painful for him.

The law in that state required physical evidence to be present in order to report abuse. Because there were no marks or bruises to justify a physical abuse case, the social worker did not call child protective services. However, she asked the client's permission to talk with his mother so that she could help him address it. When he agreed, the social worker arranged a home visit with the mother. At that meeting, the social worker and mother discussed the harm of physical punishment and alternate discipline methods. The boy reported in follow-up meetings that the hitting had ceased. In this example, the social worker attended to the value of the importance of human relationships, working with the mother of the client in order to create a healthier parent–child relationship. (See Corcoran & Franklin [1998], for more detail.)

Another basic value of the social work profession involves that of *integrity*, or acting toward people in a trustworthy manner. Yolanda was told by her field supervisor when she started at a therapeutic foster home agency that she should not tell her teenage clients that her internship would be over in May. The supervisor said, "They have a hard time trusting people, and if you tell them you'll be leaving after a year, that'll give them an excuse not to trust you." By concealing the fact that the internship represents a time-limited period, the intern is being asked to behave in an untrustworthy manner. Of note is that when clients of the foster home agency discover that it was kept from them that interns leave after a year, they may actually feel more hurt and anger, reinforcing their belief that "people are not to be trusted."

Social workers must further show *competence* in their practice and act within the bounds of their training and expertise. Shirley is a 27-year-old woman from El Salvador in her 30th week of pregnancy. She was referred to the social worker due to a sad affect, caused by the recent incarceration of her husband.

Intern: What makes you come to see me today, Shirley?

Shirley: I am really sad.

Intern: What is it that makes you so sad?

Shirley: My husband was arrested yesterday by immigration officers. He wasn't doing anything wrong. He was only working.

Intern: You must be really scared.

Shirley: I am. I want you to help me figure out what to do.

Intern: Sure, we can work together on that.

Shirley: Well, I was wondering if I could go see my husband at prison. My lawyer said I shouldn't go because I don't have papers, and the police might arrest me as well, but I don't know. What do you think? Should I go visit my husband?

Intern: I'm sorry, Shirley. I can't answer that for you. I'm not a lawyer and I wouldn't know what to do. I think you should talk to your lawyer again, or with someone that knows a little bit more about immigration law. I can give you the phone number of a Legal Aid office here in Fairfax. I also have the phone number of an immigration lawyer who takes cases like yours.

Although the social work intern has some understanding of immigration laws, she is not qualified to provide legal assistance. While willing to help the client, she makes those limitations clear to the client. The intern doesn't provide information on a subject beyond her competence, but she is able to provide the client with community resources specific to her need.

ETHICAL RESPONSIBILITIES TO CLIENTS

Beyond values and principles, standards provide more detail about professional conduct. Foremost among these standards are our ethical responsibilities to clients, but there are also responsibilities to colleagues, the agency in which we work, and to the larger society. These are all detailed in the code of ethics, but we will center here on examples of ethical responsibilities to clients that arise most commonly in practice. Recall that the ethical responsibility of appropriate termination was covered in Chapter 11. After several examples here, exercises for you to try out will follow.

Similar to the ethical value of service, a foundational ethical responsibility involves commitment to clients. The promotion of client well-being underlies all our work. Other responsibilities addressed here will be self-determination, informed consent, competence, privacy and confidentiality, access to records, and cultural competence and social diversity.

SELF-DETERMINATION: ASSIST CLIENTS TO IDENTIFY AND CLARIFY THEIR OWN GOALS

Example: Recall from Chapter 3 the case of Francine, a 20-year-old young woman with a mild intellectual disability living in foster care. As this example shows, even people with cognitive limitations should be allowed to explore their choices and options about how to improve their situation, without a practitioner telling them what they must do unless there is "a serious, foreseeable, and imminent risk to themselves or others" (NASW, 1999). Although one could argue that there was some risk in Francine taking an outing from home without informing her caregivers, the risk was likely not "serious and imminent." Further, through the use of open-ended questions, the practitioner got Francine to explore her choices and their consequences and alternative, safer ways to meet her need for independence. In this way, the intern promoted the client's socially responsible *self-determination*.

Example: An intern at a school setting formed a social-skills group for first-grade girls. The intern sent home a note to all the parents explaining what skills they would work on during the group and asking them to sign and return a permission form if they would like their daughter to participate. At the first meeting of the group, numerous students had not returned their permission forms. The intern could not postpone the start of the group because the last day at her field placement was also to be the last day of the group. Nonetheless, the intern could not allow the girls to participate without permission.

When working with clients, it is important to obtain *informed consent* so that clients understand the services provided to them and give their permission to participate. Parents have to provide informed consent for their children, since children do not have the capacity to give their consent. In this situation, the intern was able to reach the parents by phone and obtain verbal permission for the remaining students before beginning the group. The intern then sent another note home so that the parents would have a written description of the group's activities. Though not ideal, this solution was both sufficient to satisfy the school's requirements *and* the code of ethics. The permission slip seeks consent from the appropriate party. The phone calls to the parents address the students' limitations in providing documentation of consent.

COMPETENCE: PROVIDE SERVICE ONLY WITHIN THE BOUNDARIES, EXPERIENCE, AND TRAINING

Example: Mara, a masters student with little experience in the field, was asked to facilitate by herself a group in her agency with a severely mentally ill population. She expressed concern to her supervisor about leading a group when she had no experience with group work or with the population. Her supervisor told her that she could do it and that all she had to do was "trust herself." The supervisor added, "Anyway, we're short-staffed, and there is no one else to lead that group. You don't want to leave the clients without a group, do you?" What ethical values are at stake here?

Mara's supervisor seems to be appealing to the value of *service* in that "social workers' primary goal is to help people in need." However, the ethical responsibility at the heart of this scenario is *competence*, with the principle being that "social workers practice within their areas of competence..." (NASW, 1999). At this point in her internship, Mara does not have sufficient experience to facilitate a group alone. Clients are not likely to benefit, and may even be harmed, by participating in a group facilitated by a person without the skill level to conduct it appropriately. Moreover, co-leading the group with a seasoned facilitator would offer her the practice and learning she needs.

PRIVACY AND CONFIDENTIALITY

Example: A social work intern and a teacher work at a school for developmentally disabled youth. The social work intern had just had a session with her client and was chatting to a teacher about it over lunch.

Intern: I just had a crazy session with Dolores.
Teacher: Oh, you did? What happened?
Intern: She was telling me all about all this stuff that happened to her over the weekend with her family and her boyfriend. She lost her virginity to Matt this weekend. Can you believe it?
Teacher: I can't believe that.
Intern: Yeah, and then she was telling me all this stuff about her past, how she's suffered from an eating disorder and had been sexually abused when she was a kid. She's finally opening up to me.
Teacher: Wow, I never knew all that about her.
Intern: Me either. And after I saw her, I went to look through her file for more background information. I found out she has been physically abused, moved around to several homes, and a bunch of other stuff.
Teacher: Are you serious? I had no idea.

In this instance, the intern clearly violates the ethical responsibility of *privacy and confidentiality*. The intern had no reason to disclose the client's personal information to the teacher or to seek additional information in the file, just because she was curious to learn more about the details of the client's life.

ACCESS TO RECORDS

Example: Kathy is a client of DHS/Child Welfare who was mandated to undergo a mental health evaluation. At the end of a meeting with the intern, Kathy asked the intern for a copy of the evaluation, saying that she was instructed to bring it to her intake appointment to begin mandated psychotherapy. The intake appointment was in three days, and the intern had no plans to see Kathy again before the appointment. The intern read the report and believed that some of the judgments contained within it might upset Kathy. To add more pressure to the situation, Kathy said that she needed to leave in five minutes to pick up her children from school.

This scenario exemplifies the principle of *access to records*, which states that social workers "should provide clients reasonable access to records," but also holds that "social workers who are concerned that access to their records could cause serious misunderstanding or harm to the client should provide assistance in interpreting the records and consultation with the client regarding the records" (NASW, 1999).

In handling this situation, the intern recognized the conflict between the client's right to be given a copy of the evaluation and the potential for misunderstanding or harm if it was not interpreted for her. The intern recognized that she herself would not have time in this particular session—with only five minutes remaining—to sit down with Kathy to read through the report. She also recognized that she may not be the right person to review the report with the client because she did not make the judgments expressed in it and did not have competence in the area of psychological assessment. The intern proceeded by calling her supervisor, who was not available. She then decided *not* to provide the report to Kathy and said that she would follow up with her the next day. The following day, the intern learned that the agency does have a preference that mental health providers who conduct evaluations do a debriefing with the client. The intern contacted the provider to arrange this meeting, forwarded the report directly to Kathy's therapist (signed releases had already been completed), and called Kathy to let her know the arrangements that had been made. Finally, the intern documented the steps she had taken and their rationale, as directed by the ethical responsibility of access to records.

CULTURAL COMPETENCE AND SOCIAL DIVERSITY

The emphasis in this book has been about working collaboratively with clients' unique worldviews and perspectives and finding and building upon strengths, key principles when working with people from diverse social contexts (Lee, 2003). These principles are critical, as there is no formulaic way to understand culture; each individual is a composite of several dimensions of diversity (class, ethnicity/race, gender, sexual orientation, physical/mental ability/disability, immigration status, marital status, political beliefs, religion, and age). Allowing clients to stand as the experts on themselves means that we learn from them rather than prescribing what they should do or stereotyping based on one dimension of their experience. Exhibit 12.2 further offers various ways that we can make adaptations and become more culturally sensitive in working with diverse clients.

EXHIBIT 12.2: Culturally Sensitive Adaptations and Examples

Culture matching: Offering intervention in the language of the participants and/or having a member from the same culture provide services	Maria was provided services in her native language by an intern who was from Latin America.
Consultation with individuals familiar with the client's culture	Trying to understand an adult Latino male who returned to live with his mother after becoming separated from his wife, a provider spoke with a Latino colleague to understand the importance of family/interdependence vs. independence.

Outreach efforts to recruit underserved clientele	Focus groups were held at a medical clinic that provided free mammogram and cervical cancer screening to find out why services at the clinic were underused by Latinas, the barriers in place, and what may facilitate services (Corcoran, Hutchison, & Berry-Edwards, 2008).
Making services accessible and targeted to clients' circumstances	Home visiting due to transportation and child care needs of families
Provision of extra services designed to enhance client retention	At an agency that offered sexual abuse treatment to victims and their families who were primarily low income, child care was offered for younger children who were not involved in the group services.
Providing material that is written at an educational level accessible to clients	The provider may read aloud assessment instruments that clients have to complete to ensure that they understand material if clients may not be at a proficient reading level.
Cultural sensitivity training for professional staff	At a residence for women who have been released from prison, the staff received sensitivity training on prostitution, as many of the residents had engaged in prostitution.
Provision of referrals to external agencies for additional services	Latino parents who discovered that their child was diagnosed with autism were referred to a Spanish-speaking support group for parents with children with special needs.
Explicitly incorporating cultural values	Child protective services caseworkers waited until the husband in a Middle Eastern household was present to avoid pressuring his wife into making a solo decision about the welfare of their child and signing agency documents based on that decision.
Exploration of persons' experiences of racism, prejudice, and discrimination	In a school-based group intervention, a fourth-grade African American girl talked about wishing she were "white" so that she would be prettier; the group facilitators explored her and the other group members' perceptions of beauty and their experiences of internalized oppression.
Empowering strategies such as advising people of available rights and resources and helping people become advocates for themselves	Susan, an intern, advocated for services for an elderly African American woman with bedbug infestation in her Section 8 apartment.

EXERCISES

Exercise 1: What ethical value is involved in the following scenario?

An intern placed at a special education program found that many of the students were first-generation Americans. Knowing that a number of her students were diagnosed with pervasive developmental disorders, the intern created a brochure with information about local resources for children with autism and their families. Because many families have low incomes, the intern searched for programs that were free or low cost. For example, the intern found a free playground designed specifically for children with disabilities that offered a free weekend program with the National Park Service. The intern also listed information about free support groups for parents at the regional chapter of The ARC.

Exercise 2: What social work value, principle, or standard does the scenario described in Chapter 3 (the group intervention at a partial hospitalization program) address?

Exercise 3: What social work values, principles, or standards does the following scenario address?

Maria is a 32-year-old single Latina with an 18-month-old son. Child protective services (CPS) has an ongoing case with this family because of the child's low weight and failure to thrive. Maria speaks no English and is reported to have immigrated from a small village in Guatemala two years ago. Since CPS has been involved, the child has gained weight, but is still only at the third percentile of desired body weight. In a process recording, the intern stated that the purpose of the contact was to gather Maria's social information in order to better understand her family support and her motives for being in this country. The intern described Maria as "a little defensive and guarded at the beginning of the meeting, inquiring as to why I was asking questions and who else would be reading what I was writing down." The intern continued, "After letting her know that I was asking her questions about her history because I wanted to get to know her better, and assuring her that everything that she was telling me was confidential and would be seen only by myself and my supervisor, she seemed to relax a bit."

Additional question: What would be a more honest way to explain this interview process to Maria?

Exercise 4: What social work value, principle, or standard does the following scenario address?

Sabina is a 28-year-old woman from Honduras in her 34th week of pregnancy. She was referred to the social worker due to sad affect.

> **Sabina:** I am nervous today.
>
> **Intern:** Is there a reason why you feel nervous?
>
> **Sabina:** My boyfriend's wife gave me "the evil eye." I'm not feeling the same. I'm nervous.
>
> **Intern:** Besides being nervous, is there something else you feel when someone gives you the evil eye?
>
> **Sabina:** I cry a lot. I don't want to share my boyfriend with his wife, but he can't leave her. She came to the U.S. unannounced and she ruined everything.
>
> **Intern:** I see. You have mentioned several problems you are having now, Sabina. I find it helpful to work on one problem at a time, whenever possible. Which of the problems you just mentioned do you want to focus on first?

Exercise 5: What social work value, principle, or standard does the following scenario address? What ethical values might be at question here?

Sarah is a student intern at Jefferson Davis Hospital and was given a list of skilled nursing facilities and home health care agencies to which to refer discharging patients. The field supervisor cautioned the intern against recommending a particular agency for patients. However, the referral lists were topped by Jefferson Davis affiliate programs, which were also highlighted in yellow marker.

Exercise 6: What social work, principle, or standard does the following scenario address? What ethical values might be at question here?

Malika, a 17-year-old African female resident exhibits angry outbursts and has vivid nightmares, causing her to wake up screaming and crying in the middle of the night. The staff working with this individual thinks her behavior is irrational and inexcusable. Their exhaustion and frustration has led them to hold the belief that she needs to be on medication. When aggravated, many of the staff will state, "She's crazy! She needs medication," as if medication will fix all of her problems.

Malika attributes her behavior to "the devil." Similarly, Malika's mother believes that Malika is affected by spells placed on her by people jealous of their leaving Africa. Both she and her daughter believe that medication will be ineffective against "the spirits that haunt her."

Exercise 1: Identify a value of social work that you have demonstrated (with its supporting principles and standards) in your field placement.

Exercise 2: For a particular value of social work, how has the operationalization of that value been at question in a specific situation at your internship? You do not need to have personally participated in the situation—it could be an observation you have made. How could this situation have been handled in a more ethical way?

Exercise 3: Can you think of an ethical dilemma you have faced in your field placement? Describe the situation and how you responded in the space below. Be sure to include the ethical values, principles, and standards relevant to this experience. If you have not experienced an ethical dilemma, is there one you have observed?

ETHICAL DILEMMAS

An ethical dilemma occurs when a social worker is forced to choose between two or more ethics. The nature of a dilemma is that some type of conflict in ethics is present, and a clear answer does not usually present itself. For this reason, you will likely continue to feel conflicted about the situation, even after you make the best choice possible.

An additional point to make about dilemmas is that while you are trying to resolve them, you must strive to maximize other values as much as possible. Take the case of protecting client well-being. In order to keep people from experiencing imminent harm (for instance, child abuse), it may be necessary to break confidentiality. However, social workers can still act with integrity. They can inform a parent who has talked about child abuse that it will have to be reported, but they may also try to involve the client in reporting the abuse him- or herself, allowing for self-determination. Authors have elaborated upon ranking principles of social work ethics (see Barksy, 2009, and Reamer, 2006), but Exhibit 12.3 simplifies the ways to consider the ethics that take precedence over others. Examples and exercises will follow.

1. Well-being vs. confidentiality

If a person is at imminent risk of harm to self or others (e.g., suicide, homicide, child or elder abuse), then the need for survival and well-being takes precedence over rights to privacy and confidentiality. For example, Karina is a 24-year-old Latin American female in her 37th week of pregnancy. During a routine prenatal visit to her doctor, Karina seemed tired, disoriented, and underweight. She was referred to the social worker because her doctor suspected that Karina was suffering from depression. During her conversation with the social worker, Karina mentioned having hallucinations of "things moving across the table" and people talking in her ear. Karina also admitted having suicidal ideation with a plan. She had begun cutting her wrists with a knife, but changed her mind at the last minute.

As a result of this conversation, the social worker decided to send Karina to the psychiatric unit. However, the social worker could not find an ambulance to transport Karina to the psychiatric unit, so a police escort was called. While these arrangements were being made, Karina waited in an empty room for the social worker to return. Karina didn't know what was going to happen until two police officers arrived to escort her.

2. Well-being vs. laws, policies, procedures

The second ranking principle is that a client's right to well-being supersedes the need to follow laws, agency policies, and procedures. An example involves a social worker employed at a victim services police unit. After a forensic interview with 13-year-old Donna, who stated that she'd been sexually abused by her 19-year-old brother, who lived out of the home, the social worker also provided crisis counseling to the mother. After talking with both the mother and the child, the social worker assessed that Donna and

Rules	1	2	3	4
The rights on top row override the rights on bottom row	• **Well-being (survival and freedom from harm)** • Confidentiality	• **Well-being (survival and freedom from harm)** • Laws • Policies • Agency procedures	• **Self-determination** • Freedom from harm that is not imminent (for adults)	• **Well-being (survival and freedom from harm)** • Another person's right to • Privacy • Freedom • Self-determination

EXHIBIT 12.3: Ranking Principles

her younger sisters remained at risk; Donna's mother, while not denying that the abuse had occurred, was dismissive of the incidents and seemed more protective toward her son than her daughters. The social worker shared her views with both the child protective services (CPS) worker and the worker's supervisor. Ultimately, however, CPS did not open a case since Donna's mother had agreed to supervise her daughters when her son visited the home.

A few days after, Donna called the social worker to say that she was staying with her older sister, who was estranged from Donna's mother. Donna said she had run away because her mother was angry at her for reporting the abuse and had allowed the brother to come by the house when she was not home. When Donna's mother filed a runaway report, the social worker would not reveal Donna's whereabouts to the assigned police officer due to the mother's lack of supportiveness. At that point, the lieutenant of the juvenile unit became involved. He demanded that the social worker reveal Donna's location so that she could be returned to her mother. The social worker continued to refuse, explaining on what grounds she was keeping the information private. Because the social worker was employed at a police department, personnel expected her to follow the rules of the organization and work with them to solve their legal cases. However, in this case, the social worker believed her ethical commitment to client well-being trumped her having to follow police procedures.

3. Self-determination supersedes client well-being

In this third ranking principle, a client's right to self-determination trumps his or her well-being. In other words, people have the right to determine how to conduct their lives, even if it may result in *eventual* (as opposed to imminent) harm. As an example, an intern visits Ms. Werber, a 91-year-old Caucasian female with minor memory deficits, who lives independently in a continuing care retirement community. The intern has been asked to see Ms. Werber because she has refused to take her medications (which comprise 13 pills a day) for several weeks from the home support nurse. The latter service was originally requested by the client and has been taking place for the past two years. Ms. Werber tells the intern that she has lived happily for 91 years but is now "ready for God to take her life." She goes on to ask the intern to cancel the home support services for her.

The intern can promote responsible self-determination by helping the client understand the implications of her decision through exploratory questions, such as: "What is likely to happen when you stop taking your medication?" "What changes in your health will you see?" "What is likely to happen as a result?" and "Have you discussed this decision with anyone else?"

Most readers will be concerned with what may happen to Ms. Werber if she were to discontinue her medications. But because she is not at imminent risk of hurting herself or others, she has the right to make this choice. However, to further respect the client's right to *self-determination,* the intern provides her with the necessary information so that Ms. Werber can cancel the home support services herself.

EXERCISES

What ethical dilemma is present in the following situations?

Exercise 1: Stephanie's son Nate (now one year old) was put in foster care earlier in the year because Stephanie became homeless and couldn't take care of him. She was living in a shelter but left for unknown reasons. The Department of Social Services tried to get her a housing voucher, but she did not provide the necessary documents and has not completed the application. In this scenario, the caseworker and her supervisor are meeting with Stephanie to talk about her situation.

Intern: Nate has been in foster care for the last several months. Do you have any plan for him? We don't want him to stay in foster care forever. We want you to come up with a permanency plan for Nate.
Supervisor: You have several options when thinking about the plan. Option one is a relative placement. Option two is to ask the foster parents to adopt Nate. Option 3 is adoption.
Intern: Tell me about Nate's father's family. Maybe they would like to take care of him.
Stephanie: No, hell no. I don't want anything to do with them.
Supervisor: I hate to tell you this, but it is not about you. It is about Nate.
The client responds with silence.

Exercise 2: Mrs. Hall is a 33-year-old African American single parent with three children, ages 15, 11, and 7. She had been receiving TANF (Temporary Assistance for Needy Families) for the past three years since her husband deserted her. The intern writes, "During the past year, my agency made several efforts to get her a job, without success. The records showed that Mrs. Hall did not want to get a job, as she felt she was too busy taking care of her children, but the reality of the situation is that she is aware that getting a job will reduce her TANF check. I had the following conversation with her in other to motivate her to get a job." This scenario has been detailed in Chapters 4 and 5.

Exercise 3: Iris is a 16-year-old pregnant teenager in foster care because of sexual and physical abuse. She had run away from her placement and became involved in gang activity, which resulted in the death of another teenager. The CPS supervisor and Iris's guardian ad litem have suggested that the baby be taken away from her at birth. They base their decision on the psychological evaluation that concluded Iris is "antisocial" and shows little remorse for the death in which she was involved. In spite of this opposition, Iris has expressed interest in parenting her unborn child. Her foster care worker advocates for Iris to parent her unborn child because the justifications offered by the supervisor and the guardian are speculative. The social worker argues that they have overstepped their bounds as practitioners by suggesting that Iris will necessarily be a "bad parent" in the future and that it is up to Iris whether she chooses to parent her child.

CONCLUSION

The examples in this chapter have illustrated a variety of situations in which the values and principles of social work are demonstrated and also those in which ethics are at question. Although most of us espouse the values and ethics of the profession, certain situations may challenge our notions. This chapter has hopefully given you some understanding of the range of ethical dilemmas that you may encounter in beginning practice and some facility in how to act in accordance with the NASW Code of Ethics.

REFERENCES

Barksy, A. (2009). *Ethics and values in social work: An integrated approach for a comprehensive curriculum.* New York, NY: Oxford University Press.

Berg, I. L. (1994). *Family-based services: A solution-focused approach.* New York, NY: W. W. Norton & Company.

Berg, I. K., & Miller, S. D. (1992). *Working with the problem drinker: A solution-focused approach.* New York, NY: W. W. Norton & Company.

Bertolino, B., & O'Hanlon, B. (2002). *Collaborative, competency-based counseling and therapy.* Boston, MA: Allyn & Bacon.

Cade, B., & O'Hanlon, W. H. (1993). *A brief guide to brief therapy.* New York, NY: W. W. Norton & Company.

Carroll, K. (1998). *A cognitive-behavioral approach: Treating cocaine addiction.* Retrieved from http://archives.drugabuse.gov/txmanuals/CBT/CBT1.html.

Christensen, D., Todahl, J., & Barrett, W. (1999). *Solution-based casework: An introduction to clinical and case management skills in casework practice.* Piscataway, NJ: Aldine Transaction.

Corcoran, J. (2002). Developmental adaptations of solution-focused family therapy. *Brief Treatment and Crisis Intervention, 2,* 301–313.

Corcoran, J. (2005). *Building strengths and skills: A collaborative approach to working with clients.* New York, NY: Oxford University Press.

Corcoran, J. (2009). *Social work group workbook.* Boston: Allyn & Bacon.

Corcoran, J., & Franklin, C. (1998). A solution-focused approach to physical abuse. In T. S. Nelson & T. S. Trepper (Eds.), *101 more interventions in family therapy, Vol 2.* (pp. 482-486). Binghamton, NY: Haworth Press.

Corcoran, J., Hutchison, E., & Edwards, J. (2008). *Latina Breast and Cervical Cancer Screening: Attitudes of Consumers and Providers.* Council on Social Work Education, Annual Program Meeting, Philadelphia, PA.

de Jong, P., & Berg, I. K. (2008). *Interviewing for solutions, 3rd. ed.* Pacific Grove, CA: Brooks/Cole.

de Shazer, S. (1994). *Words were originally magic.* New York, NY: W. W. Norton & Company.

de Shazer, S., Berg, I. K., Lipchick, E., Nunnally, E., Molnar, A., Gingerich, W., & Weiner-Davis, M. (1986). Brief therapy: Focused solution development. *Family Process, 25,* 207–21.

de Shazer, S. (1988). *Clues: Investigating solutions in brief therapy.* NY: Norton.

D'Zurilla, T., & Nezu, A. M. (2001). Problem-solving therapies. In K. S. Dobson (Ed.), *Handbook of cognitive-behavioral therapies* (pp. 211–245). New York, NY: The Guilford Press.

Deater-Deckard, K., Dodge, K. A., & Sorbring, E. (2005). Cultural differences in the effects of physical punishment. In M. Rutter & M. Tienda (Eds.), *Ethnicity and causal mechanisms* (pp. 204–26). New York, NY: Cambridge University Press.

DePanfilis, D. (2000). How do I develop a helping alliance with the family. In H. Dubowitz & D. DePanfilis (Eds.), *Handbook for child protection practice* (pp. 36–40). Thousand Oaks, CA: Sage Publications .

Di Castelnuovo, A., Costanzao, S., Bagnardi, V., Donati, M., Iacoviella, L., de Gaetano, G. (2006). Alcohol dosing and total mortality in men and women: An updated meta-analysis of 34 prospective studies. *Archives of Internal Medicine, 166*, 2437–2445.

Dunn, C., Deroo, L., & Rivara, F. (2001). The use of brief interventions adapted from motivational interviewing across behavioral domains: A systematic review. *Addiction, 96*, 1725–42.

Dyes, M. A., & Neville, K. E. (2000). Taming trouble and other tales: Using externalized characters in solution-focused therapy. *Journal of Systematic Therapies, 19*(1), 74–81.

Fernandez, M., Iwamoto, K., & Muscat, B. (1997). Dependency and severity of abuse: Impact on women's persistence in utilizing the court system as protection against domestic violence. *Women & Criminal Justice, 9*, 39–63.

Foster, S., & Robin, A. (1998). Parent-adolescent conflict and relationship discord. In E. Mash & R. Barkley (Eds.), *Treatment of Childhood Disorders*, 2nd. Ed. (pp. 601–646). New York: Guilford Press.

Greene, G., Lee, M.Y., Mentzer, R., Pinnell, S., & Niles, D. (1998). Miracles, dreams, and empowerment: A brief therapy practice note. *Families in Society, 79*, 395–399.

Greene, G. J., Lee, M. Y., Trask, R., & Rheinscheld, J. (2005). How to work with client's strengths in crisis intervention: A solution-focused approach. In A. Roberts (Ed.), *Crisis intervention handbook: Assessment, treatment, and research* (3rd ed., pp. 62–85). New York, NY: Oxford University Press.

Hepworth, D. H., Rooney, R., Rooney, G. D., Strom-Gottfried, K., & Larsen, J. (2010). *Direct social work practice: Theory & skills* (8th ed.). Belmont, CA: Brooks/Cole/Cengage Learning.

Killick, S., Allen, C. (1997). 'Shifting the Balance'- Motivational Interviewing to help behaviour change in people with Bulimia Nervosa. *European Eating Disorders Review, 5*(1), 35–41.

Kolko, D. J., & Swenson, C. C. (2002). *Assessing and treating physically abused children and their families: A cognitive-behavioral approach.* Thousand Oaks, CA: Sage Publications.

Lee, M.Y. (2003). A Solution-Focused Approach to Cross-Cultural Clinical Social Work Practice: Utilizing Cultural Strengths. *Families in Society, 84*, 385–395.

Lundahl, B., Nimer, J., & Parsons, B. (2006). Preventing child Abuse: A meta-analysis of parent training programs. *Research on Social Work Practice, 16*, 251–262.

McCart, M. R., Priester, P. E., Davies, W. H., & Azen, R. (2006). Differential effectiveness of behavioral parent-training and cognitive-behavioral therapy for antisocial youth: A meta-analysis. *Journal of Abnormal Child Psychology, 34*(4), 527–43.

McMillen, J. C., Morris, L., & Sherraden, M. (2004). Ending social work's grudge match: Problems versus strengths. *Families in Society, 85*(3), 317–25.

Miller, W. R., & Rollnick, S. (2002). *Motivational interviewing (2nd Edition).*NY: Guilford.

Mirin, S., Batki, S., Bukstein, O., Isbell, P., Kleber, H., Schottenfeld, R., Weiss, R. D., & Yandow, V. W. (2006). Practice guideline for the treatment of patients with substance use disorders: Alcohol, cocaine, opioids. In *American Psychiatric Association practice guidelines for the treatment of psychiatric disorders: Compendium.* Washington, DC: American Psychiatric Association.

Morris, S., Alexander, J., & Waldron, H. (1988). Functional family therapy. In I. R. H. Falloon (Ed.), *Handbook of behavioral family therapy* (pp. 107–127). New York, NY: Guilford Press.

Moyers, T., & Rollnick, S. (2002). A motivational interviewing perspective on resistance in psychotherapy. *JCLP/In Session: Psychotherapy in Practice 58*, 185–93.

National Association of Social Workers. (1999). *Code of ethics.* Alexandria, VA: Approved by the 1996 NASW Delegate Assembly.

O'Hanlon, W. H., & Weiner-Davis, M. (1989). *In search of solutions: A new direction in psychotherapy.* New York, NY: W. W. Norton & Company.

Perlman, H. (1957). *Social casework, a problem-solving process.* Chicago, IL: University of Chicago Press.

Reamer, F. (2006). *Social work values and ethics, 3rd ed.* New York, NY: Columbia University Press.

Rogers, C. (1951). *Client-centered therapy.* Boston, MA: Houghton Mifflin.

Rooney, R., & Chovanec, M. (2004). Involuntary groups. In C. D. Garvin, L. M. Gutierrez, & M. J. Galinsky (Eds.), *Handbook of social work in groups* (pp. 212–226). New York, NY: The Guilford Press.

Walitzer, K., Dermen, K., & Conners, G. (1999). Strategies for preparing clients for treatment: A review. *Behavior Modification, 23,* 129–51.

Webster-Stratton, C., & Herbert, M. (1993). What really happens in parent training? *Behavior Modification, 17,* 407–57.

White, M., & Epston, D. (1990). *Narrative means to therapeutic ends.* New York, NY: W. W. Norton & Company.

Yanca, S. J., & Johnson, L. C. (2008). *Generalist social work practice with families.* Boston, MA: Allyn & Bacon.

INDEX

motivational interviewing
   guiding principles, 9–10
   decisional balance, 79–89
   resistance, managing, 71–75

National Association of Social Workers Code of
      Ethics, 6, 8, 31, 173, 181–197
Nonvoluntary (mandated) clients, 9–10, 27–30
normalizing, 34–35. *See* solution-focused therapy
Norman, B., 27

open-ended questions. *See* questions
oppressed populations, 15, 184. *See* vulnerable
      populations, social justice

privacy, 22, 186, 188, 194. *See* ethical
      responsibilities, standards
problem solving,
   process, 5–7, 9
   skills, 7, 51, 107, 134–147

questions
   hypothetical, 124, 125
   closed-ended, 10, 53–56
   future-oriented questions, 124–129
   open-ended, 7, 49–59, 139
   relationship questions, 7, 38–39, 130–131
   relative influence, 40, 41
   strengths-based questions, 90–107

records access, 186, 188–189. *See* ethical
      responsibilities, standards
reflective listening, statements, 11, 61–72, 78
reflecting statements, 11
reflection. *See* motivational interviewing, resistance,
      managing
   amplified, 73
   double-sided, 73
   simple, 72
reframing, 34, 64
relationship questions, 7, 38–39, 130–131. *See*
      questions, solution-focused therapy
resistance, managing
   agreement with a twist, 73
   amplified reflection, 73

free choice, clarifying, 74
double-sided reflection, 73
exercise, 75
shifting focus, 73
simple reflection, 72
role playing, 158–163

safety, 24. *See* home visiting
scaling questions, 129–133
self-determination, 8, 89, 134, 186, 195. *See* ethical
      responsibilities, standards
shifting focus, 73. *See also* motivational interviewing,
      resistance, managing
simple reflection, 72. *See also* motivational
      interviewing, resistance, managing
social diversity, 186, 189. *See also* cultural
      competence, ethical responsibilities
social justice, 184. *See* values
social work values, 134, 156, 158, 183–186
solution-focused therapy, 6–9, 35, 38, 46
   complimenting, 30–31, 159
   coping questions, 35
   dream question, 124
   eliciting strengths, 27
   externalizing, 40–41
   normalizing, 34–35
   reframing, 34
   relationship questions, 38
   scaling questions, 129–133
strengths-based assessment, 92–107
   biopsychosocial-spiritual, 92–98
   strengths-based questions, 90–107
summarizing, 76
sympathy, 62

termination
   building on change, 174
   evaluation, 173
   exercise, 178
   planning for, 173
   processing feelings, 174
   tasks involved, 173
   unplanned terminations, 178–180

vulnerable populations, 15